Blood Sorcery Bible

OTHER TITLES FROM FALCON PRESS

Israel Regardie
  The Complete Golden Dawn System of Magic
  The Golden Dawn Audio CDs
  The Eye in the Triangle
  What You Should Know About the Golden Dawn
Joseph C. Lisiewski, Ph.D.
  Israel Regardie and the Philosopher's Stone
  Ceremonial Magic and the Power of Evocation
  Kabbalistic Cycles and the Mastery of Life
  Kabbalistic Handbook for the Practicing Magician
  Howlings from the Pit
Christopher S. Hyatt, Ph.D.
  Undoing Yourself With Energized Meditation & Other Devices
  Radical Undoing: Complete Course for Undoing Yourself (DVDs)
  Energized Hypnosis (book, CDs & DVDs)
  To Lie Is Human: Not Getting Caught Is Divine
  The Psychopath's Bible: For the Extreme Individual
  Secrets of Western Tantra: The Sexuality of the Middle Path
Christopher S. Hyatt, Ph.D. with contributions by
  Wm. S. Burroughs, Timothy Leary, Robert A. Wilson, et al.
  Rebels & Devils: The Psychology of Liberation
S. Jason Black and Christopher S. Hyatt, Ph.D.
  Pacts With the Devil: A Chronicle of Sex, Blasphemy & Liberation
  Urban Voodoo: A Beginner's Guide to Afro-Caribbean Magic
Lon Milo DuQuette & Christopher S. Hyatt, Ph.D.
  Aleister Crowley's Illustrated Goetia
Christopher S. Hyatt, Ph.D. & Antero Alli
  A Modern Shaman's Guide to a Pregnant Universe
Antero Alli
  Angel Tech: A Modern Shaman's Guide to Reality Selection
Peter J. Carroll
  The Chaos Magick Audio CDs
  PsyberMagick
Phil Hine
  Condensed Chaos
  Prime Chaos
  The Pseudonomicon

**For up-to-the-minute information on prices and
availability, please visit our website at
http://originalfalcon.com**

Blood Sorcery Bible

Volume I:
Rituals in Necromancy

A Treatment on the Science of
Blood & Magnetics as They Pertain to
Blood Sorcery and Necromancy

**A Work By
Sorceress Cagliastro,
The Necromancer**

THE *Original* FALCON PRESS
TEMPE, ARIZONA, U.S.A.

International Standard Book Number: 978-1-935150-81-7
Library of Congress Catalog Card Number: 2011916760

First Edition 2011

The paper used in this publication meets the minimum requirements of the American National Standard for Permanence of Paper for Printed Library Materials Z39.48-1984

Address all inquiries to:
THE ORIGINAL FALCON PRESS
1753 East Broadway Road #101-277
Tempe, AZ 85282 U.S.A.
(or)
PO Box 3540
Silver Springs, NV 89429 U.S.A.

website: http://www.originalfalcon.com
email: info@originalfalcon.com

WRITTEN WITH THE INSPIRATION AND INPUT OF

My 9 attending demons, aptly named 1,2,3,4,5,6,7,8
and most powerfully, 9

in conjunction with the cautionary words
of a screeching demon child identified as Sheeg,

and the post mortem channeled words of the
7th Lubavitcher Rebbe, Menachem Schneerson
of blessed memory

DEDICATION

This book is dedicated to

Madame Curie

my mentor, who knew that the laboratory was a
lover who had no walls or boundaries

and to

the disincarnate verbal

7th Lubavitcher Rebbe, Menachem Schneerson

of blessed memory

"Blood Sorcery is the only *absolute sorcery* with no need for external tools. The only Sacred Elixir we will ever need flows within us, as the iron it harbors proves us to already be a vital part of Blood's magnificent magnetic equation."

IF I MAKE AN AGREEMENT THAT ANY BEING HAS A POWER OVER ME—THEN I AM MAKING AN AGREEMENT THAT ALL BEINGS DO.

— SORCERESS CAGLIASTRO,
THE NECROMANCER

TABLE OF CONTENTS

APPOINTMENT WITH FEAR

I accepted an appointment to meet with Fear
It was necessary to do so as Fear phones so many times,
and I could no longer avoid the calls.
Fear and I intended to meet.
I was to listen, and Fear was to read aloud a list of
limitations to which I was to heed.
Fear and I decided to meet in open air—in public,
so that everyone could witness Fear and I talking.
A location was chosen.
Fear and I would meet on the corner of Chance and Memory,
where their junction formed the Northern tip of Possibility Park.
Fear dressed for the occasion in finery, studded shirt and
big buckle shoes, a hat of pressed rabbit fur and no satchel.
A confident Fear chose to carry only a pipe and a billfold.
Fear prepared the documents, the lists, and suggested I
bring my passport
so that Fear would know for sure I was actually me, then
snatch it away confining me to one country.
Fear rose early, as I am told—as Fear shared
the importance of the event with our common associates,
stating that I am very difficult to pin down so this meeting
was vital.
Fear showed up all ready to deal with me, settling down on
the bench filled with pride of purpose,
or so I am told by witnesses who saw Fear there,
as I did not bother to attend
because Fear is irrelevant.

— *Sorceress Cagliastro, The Necromancer*

13

PREFATORY REMARKS

A Word of Caution

This book is meant for adults as it has adult content. The rituals in this book require the harvesting of the Sacred Elixir, the term I use to refer to our Blood. These rituals are not meant to be performed by minors or persons with physical or mental afflictions for which their physical or mental well-being would be in jeopardy. Blood Sorcery requires Blood and the harvesting of Blood, and the result of these events themselves lead to powerful states of mind that can cause one to feel disoriented. If you feel you are well, and stable in body-mind, then read on.

Personal Note

You won't like this book, this "grimoire," unless you enjoy learning as would an eager apprentice willing to extrapolate meaning and ritual from examples and stories. To learn Sorcery and, to put a finer point on it, to learn Sacred Elixir Sorcery, one must pull away from and uncover the method by which it is done through observation of the event.

If you are seeking a Blood Sorcery or Necromancy cook-book—a list of some ingredients to toss together and amuse yourself and impress on-lookers—this is not that book. The work in your hand functions in a prose-like way, telling stories about how the work happens in real-world time, in congress with the Science of Sorcery. Without understanding the science of who we are and how we exist in the presence of and the practice of Blood Sorcery and Necromancy, we remain at a disadvantage. I have purposefully set this book up in a way that gives the reader space to scribble thoughts amongst its pages. It is a Personal Item, a Talisman, yours and yours only to read, absorb and deface if you feel the need.

Sorcery should not have to cure over time. Sorcery is a bullet solution with the only variable being the ability of the practitioner. If you are committed to the work and fearless, not burdened with approval-seeking from others, willing to approach Sorcery as a scientist would approach research, and if you have the desire to attain what you crave without apology, then this is a work suited to your needs. If you are apologetic about success or timid about that which is necessary to attain it, put this book down and walk away.

Sorcery manuals are a curious lot. Modern ones are either diluted derivatives of more commanding works and those of antiquity lack an audience with the skill to read their sparse words and find their hidden clues. In this moment in time, this type of work should be presented as a well-constructed line drawing with ten thousand meanings. Many great directives have been given this way. For example, if you found yourself interested in the inventions and discoveries of Da Vinci, you might find it more comfortable to learn of his work through that which others have written of him. Da Vinci's famous 'Notebooks' are sketches, ideas, experimental data and lists of this and that. He presents his work in this manner because a mind of that sort which creates what others cannot would be burdened by a need to also develop the ability to make that work teachable to others. Great minds often document and share their work through their illustrations of passion. Brilliant minds often lack the pedestrian ability to transfer their materials to conventional directive, or to consider a discussion of their successes via scratched down lists with check marks and Yes or No tallied study guides. Da Vinci's notebooks present the material as a storyboard, a basic plot of how it all came to be. The question of where it went and where it can go from there is up to the reader, the next inventor, or the next Sorcerer.

Blood Sorcery is about discovery of one's own power, one's own sophistication and ability, and one's servitude to the self. Experiment is vital to the Blood Sorcerer. This is the personal exploration of the Left Hand Path.

The Left Hand Path has been described as the dark side. Oversimplified as black magic by Blavatsky, it has also been described by historian Dave Evans as practiced by those of us who reject social convention and the status quo and question religious dogma. The followers of Anton LaVey's Satanism and the Dragon Rouge have been considered to be Left Hand Practitioners as well, with their own language of necessary requirements and requirements of thoughts to be controlled by no one but themselves. To me, the Left Hand is the hand of receiving, and Blood Sorcery is about receiving that which you find to already be yours, the having of outcomes and tangibles that you perceive to belong to you. List many because if you perform this work with acuity you will have all you require.

The romance and glamour you may believe exists for Sorcerers—we who cannot stop ourselves from doing this work—is all in your mind, as this is a life without guarantees—unless the work is committed to with one hundred percent of your being. For many of us, the irony is that such a way of being leaves us living the life of an outcast, a difficulty if society and its mores are important to you. The life of a Necromancer and a Blood Sorcerer is the life of one whose rapier mind will be mocked and unappreciated for most of one's life. For these reasons we must be successful and push forward. By developing and acting on the ability to create our own living environments we achieve the freedom necessary to not look over our shoulders and to fully enjoy the decadence that is available through our actions.

Who Are We?

We are those lurking in broad daylight, those who appear to be fringe players—disenfranchised, lonely and never quite able to choose a path. Occasionally we are defiant showmen appearing to have gone so far that we have become caricatures of ourselves. The loop closes, startling the 'cog in the wheel class,' when they realize that we are exactly what we presented ourselves to be and must be taken seriously. The situation exists without compliment or complaint as no one can do this work unless this is the one true path—that path to which you cannot say "No." Blood Sorcery and Necromancy are callings. If you choose to live your calling in the shadows and that brings you joy—then delight in that way of being. If you choose to live it front and center amongst decadence and exotic fanfare, then enjoy the ride.

Who Else Are We?

We are strong players in this game. Sometimes we are vastly rich and serve as stars and leaders, gratified by the wealth and epicurean lifestyles we have hunted and captured. We are surface dwellers in spotlights and subterranean dwellers consulted as experts in matters of state, science, and other areas of great importance. We are untouchable and unapproachable, and that is part of our currency.

Who Am I?

The work I can now do is an accumulation of years of true dedication to the deceased, a willingness to place the needs of the disincarnate above those of the living, and a series of agreements, which ultimately must pay out to me in the endgame if I am to agree to make them at all. I am selfish and self-centered and protect those around me with a viper's tongue and a venom without an antidote. I am both an experimenter and an experiment, answering to my own internal thesis questions of "What else can be done? What is next?" I am unapologetic and brilliant, well read and an explorer of the processes of great scientists. My idols are non-existent as no one has yet created all that is possible. My admirations and curiosities lie in the work of Marie Curie and Enrico Fermi as neither of these great physicists knew the magnitude of their work, yet both considered the enormity of the potential and destruction their discoveries could one day produce. Although both proceeded with the language of caution, both were unstoppably driven to follow their passions.

I hold on to no belief—as I believe in nothing. I perceive each action, each moment, as pure proof of procedure resulting in evidence of existence. Love, lust, torment, joy, orgasm, hunger, anger, boredom and confusion are only proof to me that we still exist in this moment. The disincarnate walk amongst us in the same state, unfinished as they are.

TO BE UNFINISHED MEANS TO 'STILL BE'.

TO BE FINISHED MEANS TO 'BE STILL'.

The life in this work forces Sorceresses and Necromancers into an agreement to slither amongst rotted remains and sleep in their company without fear, and to spend great portions of one's life mocked and shunned. The payment comes at the moment of realization that those who shun us are not worth even a moment of our contempt, yet it takes some of us years to understand that.

The test of one's commitment to this work comes when one is called to service in moments of extreme need—then praised for one's success—and then tossed away in social disassociation. Every time I am handed untraceable cash by a law enforcement agency to work on a missing person's case, or to ask a murder victim what happened in the search for additional information, or by a major law firm to confuse the mind of the opposing counsel during their arguments, I receive this cash payment in exchange for the right they have purchased to deny any my participation or public claim for the success of my own work. I continue to do this work because families get the information, cases are solved, defendants win, so the purpose is served. Make no mistake—I am not complaining. I know through my life of work that it is irrelevant if I am credited, as those who would credit me would never be able to understand my true value. Therefore their credit to me is better served by stepping away and clearing my path toward whatever is next. That is the life of The Blood Sorcerer, the life of The Necromancer.

The original Blood Sorcery Bible, Rituals in Necromancy was handwritten over hundreds of plates with a quill pen and in ink of which nearly half of its content was my own Sacred Elixir, my own Blood. The words you are about to read are text—later typed from words written in my own hand, with no prepared notes and in my own Sacred Elixir. I have taken the liberty to expand the contents of the original version of this book in this format, as my thought process spontaneously offered new content while writing. So, if the occasional error in syntax or spontaneous story or sketch bothers you as you travel through this book, then you were not born with the capacity to see this particular opportunity and you should not read on...

> **WHEN YOU PRE-DECIDE WHAT SOMETHING LOOKS LIKE, YOU HAVE MOST CERTAINLY CAUSED YOURSELF TO NOT BE ABLE TO SEE IT WHEN IT APPEARS.**

ON THE SUBJECT OF DEATH

The questions that plague me are: What Is Life? When Is Something Really Dead? If I can still talk to a being that is dead, then is death what we have thought it to be?

Then there is, of course, my favorite question: What's Next? Maybe death isn't what we believe it is or perceive it to be. Perhaps we need to look again at how death occurs— or if it occurs at all. If death does occur then death must be an event, a moment, a date, a recordable fact. Is someone on life-support dead? Is coma death if one is not self-sustaining? Even if a coma patient can breathe on their own they will starve without the feeding tube. Isn't that—the inability to sustain life—the absolute definition of death?

On bookshelves filled with manuals of new age regurgitated observations of the human form, one sees milk teeth versions of various cultures' definitions of **life** and what it may mean to be alive. Words such as "functioning", "participating" and "contributing" are included in these definitions, connecting the concept of life to social concepts. If these definitions were to hold true, then at those periods in history a drunken stupor or the resulting lack of consciousness from a head injury would define one as being dead as it separates a person from their ability to function in society. For the purpose of my work, life and death must be able to be defined (if they prove to be definable) as stand-alone experiences devoid of reliance upon other qualifications.

I have dedicated my entire life to the exploration of death and now I am not sure it absolutely exists, except through our understanding of loss and change. I know discomfort exists, as do loss, transition, and not-aliveness (if you will)— but what does it mean to be dead?

I have been experimenting with the organs I have harvested from the food-service bullfrogs I use for mummification classes. These frogs are purchased alive, and decapitated for the buyer. In my laboratory I eviscerate them. What I have noticed is that frogs possess unusually powerful nervous systems, which results in motion even after beheading. The heart is removed, (the exact time is noted in a journal for the comparison of data noting the time between decapitation and evisceration), each time at an increased period of time. At the time of this writing, I am able to reanimate a frog heart twenty-nine hours post decapitation in the palm of my hand. My method involves the utilization of my pulse and powerful magnets. So the questions must be asked: Is this heart a dead thing, and does this experiment serve to narrow down the time of death or widen it? Does to be living mean to be autonomous? Is the heart ever alive when it is contained within the frog, or is the frog alive because the heart is beating within? I wonder if while reanimated in my hand twenty-nine hours post decapitation the heart "lives" for the first time.

The point being that after devoting my entire life to death, with the introduction of physics into my work in recent years, I find myself asking death to prove itself to me.

A NOTE ON SORCERY, SELF DELUSION & SELF-RIGHTEOUS NONSENSE

It is important to make this point—Sorcerers, stop fooling yourselves:

ALL SORCERY IS DARK

When you choose to use Sorcery to change the outcome of a situation, even when you are forcing that which you perceive to be good to replace that which you perceive to be bad (if such a delineation exists) you are enacting a manipulation, performing a change in ordinary paths—you are enacting Dark Sorcery.

I offer the following information only as an opportunity for the reader to access your own views on Sorcery and manipulation. I will soon begin sorcery on a woman who drowned her two young boys so she could reunite with her lover. I have my own personal reasons for my desire to enact sorcery upon her. When I do so she will drown like they did, experience what they experienced, and she will do so in dry air while others watch. Now reader—to address the point of good and bad and dark and light—do you perceive my desire to perform this sorcery as a good thing? A bad thing? Is she a being of dark—a human—or does she also have some light? I offer this issue—this scenario—so that you may have an opportunity to think, feel and observe your feelings on this matter of good and bad, dark and light. The discussion of good and bad is subjective and, like all subjective matter, is defined by opinion. By the very nature of the thing, it renders the outcome irrelevant to any data that will be recorded apart from the data of what you personally perceive as appropriate or important.

You must remember one *vital* fact: All Sorcery, most especially Blood Sorcery as you are sealing it with you own Sacred Elixir, is defined in the following way:

Your work is an examination of the way something is "meant" to go in its natural flow—staring that flow in the face and forcing upon it a brutally well-constructed group of purposeful lies. These lies—'re-truths' based upon your own determinations combined with the use of manipulative deception in the form of Blood Sorcery and directly applied to the situation with the express purpose of changing its out-come—is dark magic, Sorcery of manipulation.

WHEN YOU DO THIS WORK, LIFE PATHS WILL CHANGE FOREVER

Neither fate nor karma exists, and if they did (and I firmly stand my ground that they do not) they certainly would not exist around Sorcerers. You must take one hundred percent responsibility for the fact that you have willfully and without pause, forever affected the lives, paths, and perhaps even the deaths of the humans upon which you cast these deeds.

Do not depend on this notion called karma as there is no karma. The device in use here known by the term Karma is a tool used to control those amongst us who are weak and easily manipulated—played like marionettes by the very ones who know themselves that karma cannot exist. This term karma is a word played upon us so that we may self-police our actions through fear of retaliation.

So, what if it is all physics?...... It is.

What if it were all just magnetism?...... It is.

What if every Sorcery Event were an act of Sorcery Magnetism?...... It is.

Magnetism is the experience of being drawn, one to the other, through a force defined as an attraction to iron. Our red blood cells contain Iron.

Alchemical Symbols for Iron

That is why you will see the presence of iron and iron filings in my work. Each of us contains enough iron in our Blood to forge a nail. Therefore the Sacred Elixir is magnetic as it has iron and, if one works on the principles of magnetism, one is already part of the equation. We are already magnetized.

There is anecdotal evidence that early philosophers and alchemists believed that those elements which made up blood were round and smooth, allowing safe passage throughout the body, and that those elements in the surrounding world composed of iron must be coarse and sharp to catch onto that which magnetized to it. There is no evidence that there was absolute knowledge that blood contained iron at that time in history. If there was such evidence, I would imagine that the knowledge of the presence of iron in the blood combined with an understanding of magnetism would have led to much theorizing about our fascination with blood and may have led to thoughts on coagulation and scabbing. I would have also expected that there would have been experiments—not yet bound by the definitions of science—which would have bordered on Sorcery experiments. Perhaps there were, and we must continue to search for evidence of those trials and errors in a time when humans were experimented on in the open through the exploited classes.

I offer these thoughts as it behooves my readers to develop a bridge from Blood Sorcery to Magnetism early in the read, as I will refer to this connection often.

WHO CAN BE A PRACTITIONER?

Blood Sorcery can be embraced and performed by anyone with a passion for all things visceral and an innate need for more than one has. It is not for the timid. Not only because one must injure oneself to participate, but because one must make an agreement that the work at hand is an issue of Blood and Magnetism in one form or another and all responsibility lies with the doer. That commitment will make sense as you read on. One must also be willing to accept that Blood Sorcery is completely self-gratifying as all of your successes will feed your starved ego, and that is a very good thing for the person that you are. This joy in the capability of the self is vital and self-feeding. It is, in my opinion, the only path to fulfillment. If needing, desiring and ultimately achieving company, lovers, children, wealth, acclaim, successes of all types makes one a stronger person, then you will become entirely self-sufficient, never having to rely on public services for support.

There are no deities or divinities in my work. There is no higher power, no power above my own decisions and my own placement both in and of the universal magnetism of my own blood.

IF I MAKE AN AGREEMENT THAT ANY BEING HAS A POWER OVER ME, THEN I AM MAKING AN AGREEMENT THAT ALL BEINGS DO.

If you partake in that sort of worship it is entirely up to you to figure out how Blood Sorcery fits into those practices—although I will caution you and say that any fit is unlikely. You can only serve one master. Power must derive from one source if it is best controlled. If you are in an agreement that a god or a divinity of some kind has the final say or a judgment worth your consideration, or if that deity has a power over you or an agreement of behavior to which you feel bound, how do you expect to be able to harness and direct a single flow of force upon the work your are enacting?

Shared leadership or ruling never works; it is anathema to the definition of leadership.

ON MANIPULATION

Factually speaking, when you do this work you change the path of others and seal it with your own Sacred Elixir, your own Blood. It is a Sacred Elixir equation. Divinities, if they exist, in the contrary idea of co-leadership—would not, I assume, be fond of humans taking it upon themselves to harness energy and change the course of matters. To make your Blood Sorcery successful, you must take the full responsibility of outcome—a way of being not available to those who give over their power. If you accept a sense of order, give over right of opinion or accept a doctrine delivered to you, you are putting your future into the hands of some external floating genie.

To take the full responsibility for the outcome, you must also take on the exuberance and sense of power that comes with the territory. Pride is an underused resource. Although that sounds simple, if you are the sort that has a fear of success or a fear of anything substantial, this is not your ride.

If you can live with all of that—read on.

ON DIVINATION

When doing this work, if you find that you have a talent for divination, understand and accept that this is an art completely ruled out by the belief in a divinity. If an entity (thought of as a ruling body) has such a thinly veiled mind that it can be penetrated by divination, then this is a strong supporting argument for my personal choice not to accept or believe in deities of any kind. This knowledge would put you in the driver's seat—and the one driving gets to be god.

When doing the work of divination you will find the issue to be that the receiver is often less than happy to hear of the upcoming news ahead of experiencing it—unless it is all positive news. You may feel quite startled as even those individuals who make an appointment, pay for some form of divinatory Sorcery and tell you they want to hear everything you see, will become uncomfortable when you tell them the news which you discover on the horizon. Occasionally you will even get this negative reaction if what you tell them is news you personally perceive as positive. There are even those who will be upset by your revelations, as they will say you spoiled the surprise. These responses lead me to believe that most people really do just want to wallow in their current comfort zone.

In the dozens of years I have participated in this work, I have never been able to configure an absolute reason for these reactions. I do consider that perhaps the human condition requires confusion and shock as a vital component of day to day life, with a smattering of disappointment and fear. That being said, if divination is your talent, consider your audience with great care as you may tire quickly of them. Be careful not to be treated as a friend or a therapist.

ON THE SUBJECT OF YOUR COMPANIONS AND ASSOCIATES

The question to ask yourself is: How often in your life do you want to experience these exchanges with those who have some hidden agenda to use your precious time together as therapy? I have, as many do, spent portions of my life in the company of those who I find tiresome and adept only at whining, the making of excuses and the selecting of scapegoats. As I grew to gain respect, and garner veneration from those who have witnessed the unquestionable success rate of my work the ridicule has become more hidden, less overt—but it never really goes away. I find amusement in the time they waste amongst themselves dissecting my persona and my work, looking for cracks in the armor and loose shingles on the roof. It reminds me of the comment that the devil's best work has been convincing man he doesn't exist.

TALK ABOUT ME AMONGST YOURSELVES.

TO DO SO MAKES ME EVEN MORE TANGIBLE.

SORCERESS CAGLIASTRO, THE NECROMANCER

ONE CLEAR, NON-NEGOTIABLE DIRECTIVE:

DO NOT SHARE THIS BOOK.
IT IS A TALISMAN.
IT CAME TO YOU
BECAUSE IT IS YOUR TIME TO READ IT.

You should anoint this book with your Sacred Elixir.
Sign your name somewhere inside, prick your finger
and smear your Sacred Elixir on your name.

Once you do that, then and only then is this book yours.

BLOOD FOR MAGNETS

What can I do but love you?
I began to worship you
and a horizon unveiled the irony, as if I worship you
and you are in me
then my ego is fed.
What if I loathe you?
degrade you?
Yet find that I crave you
I am bound to you
As one is Iron for Magnets
There is enough metal in each of us to make one full nail
But what would I hammer together?
This cannot be a battle as it could only be a civil war
And I do not wish to fight amongst myself, my cities, my own
polarities.
I can only stand in awe each time you appear
Startled for a moment, as are we all,
and so it is the human condition to do so.
The question plagues me though—
How do I stand beside you even as you live within me?
Now as you stand beside me defining that which I already am,
A force pulled onto myself,
Unnatural in poetry, completely reasonable in anatomy

CREEDS

A Necromancer must have a creed. The Disincarnate can enter your life anywhere and at anytime. Death will not defend you or respect your privacy. Do not expect the disincarnate to respect your privacy if you have not made agreements with Death. A Creed creates an expectation of good behavior from the disincarnate, and they can reap rewards only through keeping the agreements of the Creed. For the disincarnate, the reward they seek is your willingness to communicate. Once you open an Eternal Portal, they will attempt to force themselves upon you by trickery and events they assume will cause fear in you, until you acquiesce. They have been doing this for, perhaps, centuries and you are new to this. Prepare yourself to be tricked, lied to, played and basically raped in the underworld.

MY CREED

This is my agreement......

I enter into this work with death
with no relationship to fear.

I enter into this work embracing death like a lover—
revealing myself and my intentions to death—
giving death comfort and a place to be.

I have replaced any fear with raw passion for this work.

I am death's mother, queen and consort.
I am the carrier of death's melancholy and ecstasy
and am openly desirous to know death in all of death's
forms, shapes and nuances,

and they may all attend me—and I they—as a lover and
as dusk enters night.

I shall never force my way into death's bed,
but neither will I decline any invitation.
We—death and I—are at each other's disposal
and we both acknowledge that the seriousness of this
agreement yields that even one intentional break of this
agreement leads to a dissolving of this creed.

I am Sorceress Cagliastro—The Necromancer

ARE YOU WILLING TO MAKE SUCH AN AGREEMENT?

The Writing of—and
Interment of—Your Creed

You will need to write your Creed. It is a control method, a
contract of sorts, and contracts keep relationships on track.

Place no fewer than seven drops of the Sacred Elixir from
your writing hand into your ink. Write your creed with a nib
or a quill. Points in your Creed should address Death
directly as if Death is a single entity. Write down many
thoughts before you complete your Creed. After it is written, put it away for a day and look at it the next day. Make
changes if you desire. It is best to re-write it in your own
Elixir but it takes a significant accumulation to do so. Accu-
mulate and refrigerate or freeze it until you have enough.

When you have collected enough Sacred Elixir, combine
it with seven drops of ink. Write your Creed on parchment
and leave it for three sun-downs. After three sun-downs, if
you are absolutely sure of its content, take it to a cemetery
and bury it, words facing downward, in a hole on the oldest
grave you can find of someone who died too young. A very
old grave of a child would be perfect. Let it rot into the
earth.

(Note: Please remember that unlike any other type of
Sorcery, Necromancers have very few—if any—accessories

or components. The ones we do have most likely must be able to rot into the earth.)

Next I suggest you visit that grave from time to time or another grave of one who has died before their time. Bring lancets and make three incisions in the bottom of each foot.

Stand over the grave and allow your feet to bleed into the soil beneath your feet. Take in the sorrow and leave your sorrows there. You must be with death, seek it, feel it, and discover it over and over again. You must cut your feet many times and bleed into many graves, burying a part of yourself each time. You must lay down on graves, take in the experience of death. You must find ways to cry—mix your tears with Death. You must sleep in mausoleums to breath Death in while you sleep. Keep your guard down, to build trust. If you cannot trust Death, then you cannot conquer fear.

THE BEGINNING: THE SACRED ELIXIR

Dearest Sorcerers, the only Elixir you will ever need flows within you at all times. Your greatest weapon and asset will never leave you. That should bring comfort to you in this quest for Sorcery skills. The evidence is pulsing within your vessels, racing within your veins and arteries, passing two types of Sacred Elixirs, crossing paths forever, in a ceaseless effort to be one whole entity and balance your world. Yet these two bloods are the very definition of conflict. You, Sorcerer, are here to exploit and unbalance...choose and decide for yourselves what is acceptable to you, what is righteous, as all is already possible...

Readers...

You may travel the earth to find the most perfect oil, pressed in just the right way, an absolutely glorious ratio of herb to liquid. With the erotic touch of a lover's hand you will store the bottle as if it is a Sacred Relic, stroking it, breathing it in, using it sparingly, anointing candles with its intoxicating lubrication. When the process is complete you will wait quietly in the cool darkness for results from this seductive foreign object—foreign to your body, a visitor to your being. You will wait and wait and wonder, yet you deny, ignore or question the use of the one and only perfect Sacred Elixir within which waits for, begs for, your attention. Learn to love it, crave it and utilize its overtones, inhale it with the same curious sensuality brought to the greatest and sweetest patchouli or violet. Use tiny glistening amounts of it, smeared and startling, greater than the earth color of myrrh or the rich green vetivert. It is liquid ruby.

DECORUM AND PRIVACY

The Sorcery you seek is already in place, taking harbor in your arteries and veins, coming and going—continuously working. Participating in the exploitation of momentum and attraction is the task of this living oil. It belongs to you. No one can govern it or command it aside from you, as it is at the same time within you and defining you all at once.

I caution those of you who feel the need to discuss your work with others, especially for the seeking of debate. You cannot win or lose a debate on Sorcery because there is not one to be had, as there is no dogma to contest and no deity to critique. Debates strengthen the point for the debater as no one can really change the mind of others. A debate on Sorcery is a simple thing. It works or not, and if your sorcery does not yet work you are in no position to debate it.

Just as your Sorcery does, your Blood belongs to you. Do not allow anyone to tell you that you do not have the right to harvest your Blood and use it as you see fit. All other potions—useful in their own rite and lovely to have, enjoyable and inspiring to the senses—are delicious props. These great scented oils are the jewelry without the warm skin to rest upon—alone and inactivated by the Sacred Elixir, they are toys of the fearful and unready, a crutch in a world of distractions.

Enjoin your Sacred Elixir by adding drops of it to your scented potions, and wear it yourself or use it to control another. There is a great deal of power in it, a carnal, primal imprint of you will be set in a deep place of the being upon whom you may find the need to smear it.

SACRED ELIXIR: ARTERIAL

Arterial Sacred Elixir is bright red, pushing with power to a swollen organ or a filled breast—begging to be taken, used, released of its burden—sent out to implore the needy to live through its message. It carries Iron, the destination of the magnet, the forward force of motion, leading the path to magnetic fulfillment. Arterial Blood is both the seeker and the sought.

"Take me," it whispers as it passes through dark channels bringing life, reinventing transgressions by breathing new life into them, demanding acknowledgement for its ability to give this breath, to give life, to ward off Death. Arterial Blood carrying Iron is the warrior chariot for oxygen. This collaboration allows for life to continue, to be sustained. Arterial Sacred Elixir crowns itself the Elixir of life, the Elixir of the living. Use it when life is just about to be taken, one moment away—where a breath will change the course of the death at hand. Blow it in the face of death.

It is the Arterial Sacred Elixir sought after by the great icons of Sanguine feeding, fresh and breathing, but that is an aside as this is not a work discussing the culture of the Vampyre. Arterial Sacred Elixir is crimson, delicious, ripened and flowing warm and alive from the being taken in hand. A viscous wine using its power, holding its life force over us, causing even the most robust amongst us to perceive of a moment of submission; reminding us that our finite mouths crave sucking at the portal meant for giving life.

Dare we harness and use this Arterial Sacred Elixir, this liquid diamond, for our own gain, our own purposes, to bait the disincarnate into communication and bend death, to lure those into servicing us in the desire to fulfill our will? Of course we do, that is the primary connection between Blood Sorcery and Necromancy. Douse yourself in Arterial Blood and they will come to you as hungry fish to the hook, remembering the smell, remembering what it felt like to be alive. But take care, as without the proper skills you will not be able to fend them off and they will feed from you to have one more moment of cherished contact.

Arterial Blood is a Sorcery implement when set apart from its vessels, spilled and causing chaos in even the most jaded assassin. Thieved from the very host it was meant to sustain, it takes on a new purpose, even as it flashes a red warning that some life has been spilled away. I imagine even the Ripper jolted at first release each time he began his work. If there is any cultural universal, it is that we as humans react in a way to the appearance of blood that is separate and apart from the manner in which we react to any other matter.

Arterial Sacred Elixir is self-baiting, hanging on a hook of iron already implanted within. The disincarnate can smell it, and they will show up, because they want to remember what it was like to pulse. The Arterial Sacred Elixir and the disincarnate will now submit to a new master when appropriately utilized—the Blood Sorceress.

DRAW THIS SACRED ARTERIAL ELIXIR AND PROCLAIM "MY VIAL IS FULL, THERE IS WORK TO BE DONE."

SACRED ELIXIR: VENAL

Venal Sacred Elixir, the bruised and beautiful swill flowing through your veins, bluer and burdened, carries dirty remnants away from hidden trunks filled with that which is already spent. No metal travels with it as it carries no need to breathe. It is the Blood of the morning after.

Venal Sacred Elixir, the 'Elixir of the scent of death' cleaning out organs—and hiding history, swifting away dirty secrets and stories—sickened azure with blue pollutants, its red darkened to the appearance of a bruise—hinted blue with its charges—yesterday's transgressions in tow. Venal Elixir's goal is to return to the pulmonary arteries, in search of the true destination—the lungs—the oxygen—the breath of life where it will be cleaned and be the absolute subject of Corporeal Necromancy. To remove death and return life is Corporeal Necromancy, and it happens every minute of the day and night in the center of your circulatory system, right at this moment, as you read this, your body is the Necromancer…as in real time at that junction Venal Blood is raised from the dead. It is gasping and anoxic representing the nearly dead, the barely definable moment of Death, the last search for escaped breath. It is drunken, rotten with activity, stinking of whisky, bereft of all sweetness, carrying urine, waste, feculent miscreants and discarded malfeasance, both intentional and otherwise.

Not bad, nor evil, just truthful—evidentiary—gathering indications, proving rumors and revealing the recent tales, torments and movements of the host. Do you dare use this Sacred Elixir, this piss in ritual? It has many purposes……

THE POOL FROM WHICH YOU DRAW: IT IS ALL PHYSICS

The reason this tome—this grimoire if you will—is called the *Blood Sorcery Bible: Rituals in Necromancy*—is because it represents my work, my way of life, and that is the work of the Sacred Elixir, the work of the Blood Sorcerer. **I have no intention of getting it right or wrong here in this book, I have only the intention of presenting the material based on the experiences of using these methods.**

> **BLOOD SORCERY, BY DEFINITION, IS THE USE OF THE SACRED ELIXIR, MORE OFTEN THAN NOT ONE'S OWN, APPLIED TO AN ACT OF SORCERY TO UTILIZE ITS PROPERTIES AS A CATALYST AND SIGNIFICANT CONTRIBUTOR OF THE MAGNETIC EQUATION IN THAT PARTICULAR ACT OF SORCERY (WHICH I REFER TO AS A SORCERY EVENT) TO MANIPULATE A CURRENT MOMENT AND ENACT A VERY PARTICULAR OUTCOME.**

Much of the Sacred Elixir you draw from your body via syringe or lancet will most likely be Venal Sacred Elixir—so when doing ritual Sacred Elixir Sorcery, you are already in the presence of the dead and dying by the materials in your hands. This is why we direct our work at our weakest point, then bring it back to life, fixing the weakest link. That procedure explains how this work is naturally bent toward the

inclusion of Necromancy. As Death is indicated by exsanguination, Death is invited each time you insult your skin
and breech it for the purpose of releasing the Elixir. At that
same time that you are one drop closer to Death, your body
is responding by making more life, producing red blood
cells, as you are a living portal. The drops of shed Sacred
Elixir which are harvested are out of your body and can no
longer promote your life. The outcome is that Death is in the
room. That is the link between Blood Sorcery and
Necromancy.

**USE THIS SACRED ELIXIR IF THE DISINCARNATE
ARE YOUR INTENDED AUDIENCE—IF YOU DESIRE TO
BE A PRACTITIONER OF NECROMANCY, YOU ARE TO
UTILIZE THE SACRED ELIXIR. THE OUTCOME WILL
OFFER PROOF, A FURTHER INDICATION THAT THIS
WORK IS A PERFECT COMBINATION OF SACRED
ELIXIR SORCERY AND NECROMANCY.**

Note: To go further in the art of Necromancy, to actually
raise the BODIES of the dead, (a **method** of Corporeal
Necromancy known as Lifting) you will have to douse yourself in Arterial Sacred Elixir when you begin the work as the
scent of life is irresistible to them. If you seek audience with
the decomposing you must smell like that which will bait
them. I will discuss this later in a chapter called "Corporeal
Necromancy". Dousing yourself in Venal Blood will allow
you to walk amongst them, not unnoticed, but disguised,
perhaps not to be consumed.

The following is a Personal comment, stated after a
Necromancy Ritual with four invited students. It is intended
as a warning…as rituals can become more than intended if

the work at hand is demanding additional comments in order to deliver the intended outcome.

"DO YOU REMEMBER, MY STUDENTS? I DREW IT WITH YOU. I HAVE EVEN INGESTED YOUR PLEASURE IN A MOMENT OF SORCERY DEBAUCHERY AND NOW YOU ARE, AS A RESULT OF YOUR WEAKNESS FOR ME, THE WEAKER ONE, THE FOOL NOW AS I SPIT YOU INTO A VESSEL... NOW I HAVE YOU TO USE AGAINST YOU IN WAYS YOU CANNOT IMAGINE. YOUR DNA ENTANGLED WITH MINE, AND NOW TO SERVE THIS RITUAL I EXTRACT IT AND USE IT TO KEEP OR DISCARD YOU AT MY WILL."

Treat these words as a Warning: be very careful where you leave your "Biologicals", most especially Venal Sacred Elixir and Semen. Others may know of its value and use it. There are many disciplines that use biologicals in their own way. Anyone who has your Venal Sacred Elixir and any talent in the world of Sorcery can find you and affect you. Venal Sacred Elixir has a specific fingerprint and it is the carrier, the host's carnal calling card, an actualized biological GPS. It is the azured Sacred Elixir of the disincarnate and the recent path of the host when released, no longer bound by location, in its most putrid and informative state, the Elixir of the dead—the story teller—the tracking device. Your scent, your story and your vulnerabilities are forever imprinted upon it. Do not leave it lying about.

MAGNETS:
CONNECTING BLOOD TO PURPOSE

I have created an area called The Surface, which is covered with extraordinarily powerful magnets of a very particular type. I refer to this placement of magnets as The Surface, and it lives at The Platform. Both of these are discussed at the end of this book.

The magnets are large, no smaller than six by ten inch blocks. I use these powerful magnets as a catalyst to connect "Blood to Purpose." The magnets I now use have lived, frozen inside blocks of Sacred Elixir that I accumulated over time. Each magnet spends a year in this frozen state and, before it is used, the Elixir is allowed to melt away slowly under a glass bell onto a glass dish, revealing the magnet. The Sacred Elixir which has melted away, is flaked and used as an additive in ink. (You will find the explanation of flaking as you move through this book.) This deep freezing is not a simple process, but one that is necessary to make the connection between Blood and Magnets. This particular kind of magnet will absorb vital energy from the Blood which encases it, enhanced by the freezing and thawing. Explore the use of magnets and how they effect the outcome of your Sorcery Events. They are very powerful catalysts. I have done extensive work with magnets and everything you are reading here is the result of experiments and reproduced results. To see The Surface in action you will have to schedule a trip to The Platform (details at the end of this book). This is the Science of Sorcery.

KNOW WHO YOU ARE

Sacred Elixir Sorcerers............
                    You know who you are, read on......
                    as for the rest of you......

Others who are reading this, it is my most sincere desire that you know who you are **not**. Most will read this tome—this Grimoire—this Science of Sacred Elixir Sorcery blueprint—fantasizing about the work at hand. You will never raise a needle or lancet to your frightened flesh, never draw a dram of your Sacred Elixir—but you will wish for a moment, with a coward's breath, that you could find the courage to do so. The magnetics within you crave the actions your type of being will never provide. You will dress and pose the part as you perceive it to appear, but you will never carry the role, never take the job. That's just fine; read on to fulfill the fantasies in your mind, or in your video game, or your social networking avatar.

But you know that should you actually attempt Blood Sorcery, judgment and fear will grasp you all at once. You will immediately suppress it with a faux bravado or deluded belief that you are above these thoughts and practices, that you—somehow—have evolved. Your convenient social consciousness, some vegan nonsense you recently read, or some ideology that humans have evolved into greater beings in the age of technology will kick in and you will be appalled at the thought of opening your tepid skin and releasing your Blood for the purpose of Sorcery. If you are so 'evolved' in this way then why have you read this far into this work? If you have suppressed your primordial urges why do you only read this book in the seclusion of your own home? You will pretend that this is a cultural exploration or some such excuse. Others of you will recoil in fear and the most bantam amongst you will judge me directly, trying to create an impression of this writer as a costume shop wizard or sideshow fortune-teller. Some will decide this is a work of fiction—whatever gets you through the night.

I offer a word of caution to the group of most fearful ones who somehow came into possession of this book with the intention to know us better and infiltrate. Know that if you pursue us or propose to possess a trait or object that we desire, one of the capable ones amongst us will someday steal your Sacred Elixir or other biological when sniffing out your weakness, as you are so easy to penetrate. You will be grazing with the herd and one of us will require the Elixir of another for a Sorcery Event and you may not even know that it has happened—as we are Sorcerers not Vampyre. Your bit of Sacred Elixir was only needed for the work. You won't even know it is missing...

Thank you in advance......

THE BODY DIVIDED: SELF VIVISECTION

For centuries, the human body has been considered by anatomists, philosophers, spiritualist, deviants, murderers, priests and healers to be a living diorama—a sure gathering of points and locations collected to create the whole. I say it is just the opposite. The human form is a gathering of rooms, stacked in a way to represent a great and complex character. Each room holds an iron floor, a story, a place, a purpose, meaning, revulsions, truths, lies and vulnerabilities. Each room has a separate door in and a door out. **Sorcerers keep guards in these rooms, and those who are not Sorcerers do not.** There is no need for extended discussion on this structure as there should be little confusion or chaos in this matter.

In my interpretation of the human whole being, this great "entire of this being" is meant to come together to create a unique focused, functioning element, a "one"—a single walking agreement balancing these rooms with a purpose—to supply a life of limitless sorcery to the being itself. Its internal structure of "life renewing death renewing life" is not a cycle as it is all happening at once in real time. The individual sees itself as boxes of whatever it desires and **strategizes the methods by which to reorder these boxes** into a sentence—a scenario of already delivering the desired prize. This discussion of boxes is advanced for this moment, and my most learned and cherished students know it well. The secret of the reordering of rooms begs to be served discretely, as it is one of the five final functioning skills of the Sorcerer and not one to be toyed with at this juncture. **This book addresses only the first of the five great skills, the**

knowing of the Sacred Elixir. Just know of the rooms and read on, suspending disbelief like a child watching Houdini on stage for the first time. That innocence is power as it lets the information in without the stranglehold of judgment.

At this point in history, most of the work on this subject of the body divided is derivative, by which I mean that a study on how sections of the body contribute their energies both individually and as part of the whole comes from other sources. For the purpose of achievement and attainment through Blood Sorcery those revisited works are all anathema to the endgame. I am going to tell you a new story about the cities of your body and what they contribute to Sorcery Events.

Overworked materials gathered about chakras, meridians, pressure points and other physiology by which we divide the human body into convenient sections relate the information to physical and emotional wellness as coming from those authors' points of view on what wellness is. Save them for the acupuncturists as they serve only that noble art. For the Blood Sorcerer they are useless. The only knowledge of anatomy you will need in order to do this work is that of the circulatory system—to avoid puncturing major vessels.

MY DEFINITION OF WELLNESS IS UNIQUE. I BELIEVE WELLNESS IS *HAVING* AND THE FULFILLMENT ONE GETS FROM THE *HAVING*. IF ONE HAS WHAT ONE WANTS, ONE IS FULFILLED AND UN-WELLNESS IS NOT PERMITTED ACCESS TO THE SELF.

If my definition feels oversimplified for you, then you are not ready to know that you deserve to have that which fulfills you. This work, this Sorcery, is a route to wellness through manipulating that which would not happen had you not interceded and created that which must happen. Blood Sorcery is the work of **'having'**. Living within one's own definition of beauty is curative. Blood Sorcery delivers through purposeful, unapologetic manipulation and directed magnetism resulting in the inevitable epicurean-inspired, driven sense of power.

LIVING WITHIN ONE'S OWN DEFINITION OF BEAUTY IS CURATIVE.

Any *deviation* from that path leads to the *decline* of wellness.

UNDERSTANDING THE CONTRIBUTION OF THE SACRED ELIXIR AS DRAWN FROM VARIOUS BODY PARTS AND SECTIONS AS THEY PERTAIN TO MATTERS SUCH AS HEALING IS NOT MY WORK HERE *BECAUSE A PERSON IN THE STATE OF WELLNESS DOES NOT NEED HEALING.*

When someone asks me to do a healing I tell them I will do a realignment, removing facades of humble posturing and humility, and creating a state of desire for more living. If they grasp that concept and let me do the work, then they will be fine.

My intention is to discuss the power of these realignments as they pertain to harvesting The Sacred Elixir, Blood, the fuel for Sacred Elixir Sorcery to provide 'having' which results in wellness.

> **I OFFER YOU A WAY OF LIFE THAT REPROGRAMS YOU TO WANT TO HAVE MORE, TO BE UNAPOLOGETIC ABOUT IT, AND TO SEEK THE BEAUTY OF HAVING AND THE HAVING OF BEAUTY.**

My data on this subject is not derived from any source other than my own experience. The information I present here is based entirely on trial and error of usage of the Sacred Elixir in matters of Blood Sorcery. Additional and occasional contributions are figured into this data by Sacred Elixir Sorcerers who have made every effort, at my asking, to experiment and report which areas of the human body produce the best sample of the Sacred Elixir as they correspond to the Sorcery at Hand.

Blood Sorcery happens in real time. A student of mine did the slicing of the palm (which I will present in a later section) and the home of the man who raped her burnt down not three days later. I tell you this because Blood Sorcery is a balance, a pure equation of one to the other. Blood Sorcery is **CAUSE DRIVEN EFFECT**. Think of it as:

+**CAUSE**—I performed this act
+**EFFECT**—and the weight of it resulted in a direct balance to justice

If you steal from me and I use Blood Sorcery to retaliate, you will experience loss. If you rape someone, you have taken the seat of their being—their "land of self"—and your home will burn to the ground. That is not magic, it is not witchcraft, it is not karma: it is Blood Sorcery.

LET US BEGIN WITH SORCERY EVENTS

Sorcery Events and Their
Accompanying Harvest Sites

This section is constructed to reveal many of the areas in the body from which the Sacred Elixir is to be harvested in order to perform and complete the work at hand. Some of the Sorcery Events in this chapter list more than one option for harvest sites with slightly different angles of approach. The specific areas within each Sorcery Event have their own properties, and their explanations follow each listing. Use the one that represents the *greatest weakness or deficit you are experiencing* when choosing an area of harvest. Unlike conventionally used superfluous white light magic nonsense, we are not interested in strengthening the area that is already the most efficient. This is not about floating genies and goddesses and circles of supportive buddies. This is about harvesting your Blood for the purpose of creating change. Letting yourself die a little to renew stronger and more capable, and having that which you request for yourself.

You are alone in this work and it is best that you understand that early in the practice of Blood Sorcery. If working on a detractor, find their **weakest** structure and hit there first. This may feel contradictory to the natural desire to break the strongest link. Breaking down the weakest link weakens the whole more and more, creating more weak links and your sorcery becomes a flesh-eating virus to the total being. This breakdown leaves your target in a manner of being such that they are expecting yet another uncomfortable thing to happen as they begin to wear the mantle of that defeated attitude. Eventually this new posture destroys your target, leaving them hopeless. I don't believe in hope as I feel it is vague and shows powerlessness, but it is more than likely that your detractor/opponent believes in it, as most people do.

GOAL

As Blood Sorcerers—exploiters of the Sacred Elixir—we are interested in *exposing the weakest point in our process and strengthening that area* so to achieve strength in our entirety. That being said— exploiting the weakness of a DETRACTOR is also effective. Learn to find the weakest structure and hit there first.

The flip side to this strategy is for yourself; strengthening the weakest element makes the whole machine run more efficiently. *That is how to build great Sorcerers.*

Procedure note on harvesting locations: at no time should multiple areas be used for one single Sorcery event unless the directive to do so is included.

You may be saying, appropriately so at this point: "I have the Elixir. Now what?"

General Uses

This is a brief comment on the generalized methods of using the Sacred Elixir. You will see that each of the Sorcery Events in the next chapter have additional or recommended methods beyond those listed here.

Generally speaking, choose a way that best serves the task at hand, using criteria such as degree of intention, availability of materials, severity of the act (specifically as your choices pertain to justice and revenge Sorcery), and finally, strategize about which actions are necessary to gain personal access to materials, etc.

Consider this the short list of methods.

The Sacred Elixir at the very least may be used in one of the following ways:

• Smeared across a photo or a representation of the target individual(s) (the 'intended' from this point forward)
• Used alone or as an additive to ink with the purpose of drawing sigils or writing a poem of intent (please be graphic in your writing as this is not the place for reserved behaviors)
• Added to grave dirt or placed into the ground of a grave or the stone of a mausoleum which holds an individual who represents an aspect of the work. It will bait them into helping you in your endeavor
• Added to the FLAME of a candle so that heat becomes a catalyst in the Sorcery
• Placed into food or drink, either yours or that of another (consensual or non-consensual)
• Left on your ALTAR TO YOURSELF as a reminder of the work at hand
• Slashed from your palm with the intention of revenge or justice
• In Sex to create possession either of complete servitude or to incite demonic possession
• To reanimate an object

• To possess an object (such as a doll) with a demon

The following are areas for Harvest based on specific Sorcery goals. I refer to these combinations as "Sorcery Events", as the term "spells" takes on a lighter and more trivialized connotation and produces an affect of boredom in me. I am stimulated by well-written Sorcery Events. I am rattled, moved and inspired by the desire to seek extraordinary language for use in place of common day statements. Spells are for witches and animated films. Sorcery is the stuff of "magnificence"—a word with a deep and obvious association to magnetics.

All of the following can utilize the above-mentioned methods as well as the expanded additional methods which are offered specifically for the following Sorcery Events.

The following is a small sample—thirty to be exact—of Sorcery Events. The possibilities are endless. My students learn hundreds of combinations to effect the manipulation needed to attain their goals. They get what they want and I am proud to see them gratified.

THIRTY SORCERY EVENTS
AND HOW TO READ THEM

Each Sorcery Event is numbered and titled, followed by the location(s) from which to harvest the elixir and then the Procedure itself. For Sorcery Events with more than one option, please read the entire Event before beginning. Prepare all materials so that you can utilize the Sacred Elixir immediately whenever possible.

SORCERY EVENT #1: To Heighten Sorcery Abilities

Heart—(draw from a small cut on your chest closest to where the heartbeat is felt to be strongest) To address weakness which lies in the area of a lack of passion or commitment

Genitals—A lack of connection to ancestry may cause interruption in the Sorcerer's ability to pursue these materials. Genital blood, used in this way, can restore this connection.

Menstrual Sacred Elixir—(can be used by either gender if available) If there is present a fear of time constraints or whether or not Sorcery is appropriate for this individual. I refer to this as answering the question: Are you a Blood Sorcerer?

PROCEDURE 1—There are several ways to use the elixir for this Sorcery Event:

Any of these Elixirs can be added to ink. To do so, add them to a black ink, preferably one with mercury, and using a hide or parchment from an animal and a freshly cut quill, write the details of that area in which you seek an increased ability. Take the document and wear it over your heart for three days and nights, then bury it at the grave of someone who has achieved something you consider extraordinary. I have left such 'notes' buried in shallow holes in several of the graves of the individuals I have admired. When you are at the graveside, remember to put at least three drops of your Sacred Elixir into the ground from the same location from which you chose to harvest for this event. Take something from the grave for your altar. Place it upon a layer of iron filings.

PROCEDURE 2—There is Demonwork on this; see the "Demonworks" chapter, Sorcery Event #1.

SORCERY EVENT #2: To Raise Passions and Invoke Desires in Self and Others

Inner thighs—If your own passion is at question.

PROCEDURE—This is for both general and sexual passions. Extract three drops of the Sacred Elixir from each thigh and put the six drops in red wine. Drink the wine. This Event is best completed if you engage in something you consider sexual while the wine is still being digested within your body.

Behind Left Knee—If you feel there is duplicity afoot blocking passion

PROCEDURE—Make an incision, roll a candle in the Sacred Elixir directly from the incision making sure to coat the wick, let the Elixir dry on the candle and crust on the incision. (Candle colors are irrelevant as we seek only the catalyst of heat and fire here.) Directly ask the appropriate person if there is any duplicity afoot *while* the Elixir dries and scabs. No matter what their response, do not answer them as this is an inquiry as part of a Sorcery Event, *not* a conversation or debate. Based on the manner in which you asked the question, hang up, walk away or stop texting or emailing before they answer. The Sorcery Event only requires that you convey the **question** to the person at hand. Whisper the question into the candle and light it. As the Elixir burns, the truth will present itself clearly in another's error or admission in real time.

Between Navel and Pubic Area—If the passion of another specific person is in question in terms of the very nature of their ability to show passion to you, and cultivating that aspect is the work at hand

PROCEDURE—Place some of a gathered 'no fewer than seven drops' of the Elixir on your inner left wrist and on new bedding. Share the new bedding with the person in question. The results will show you if passion is possible and sustainable between the two of you.

SORCERY EVENT #3: To Let Go

Right Palm—You have done all the other mental/emotional work and you just need the final push.

PROCEDURE—Cut a small incision in the part of your palm closest to your wrist (but still on your palm). Join it to your middle finger on your left hand. When there is sufficient Elixir on your finger, touch it to a piece of stone chipped from a crypt and then bury the stone in the grave of an infant. Stay awake until you cannot stand any longer. Sleep where you fall until you awake naturally. You will awaken free of the hold that was upon you.

Arches of Feet—You are only beginning the process of letting go and seek direction and stamina as they pertain to strategy.

PROCEDURE—Cut incisions into the ball of your left foot and the heel of your right. Stand on the grave of someone you believe to have been a Sorcerer or a strategist. Bring yourself to tears. When you can cry no longer, walk away. In two sunsets you will know that which you did not know before and your strategy will be clear and based on the new information.

Under Right Breast—Seeking stamina on the emotional front as you are beginning the work of letting go, when you know you have to but you don't want to.

PROCEDURE—Seek a teacher for this rite or contact me directly as the amount of Sacred Elixir is crucial and the procedure should not be done alone.

SORCERY EVENT #4: To Develop or Enhance an Ability to Study

Right Jaw—To remove self-imposed distractions.

PROCEDURE—Make a small puncture at the back of your jaw (in the face area, *not underneath* your jaw) and use the Sacred Elixir in ink as mentioned in the "General Uses" section in the previous chapter. When you are studying keep quill and parchment nearby and write without thinking. That which blocks you will reveal itself and disappear.

Tip of Left Ring Finger—To remove distractions of others.

PROCEDURE—Cut an X into the pad of this finger. Use the X shape to make a mark (as if using a stamper) in a new writing journal and also in a respected book (respected by you). Re-open the wound for three days and do exactly the same thing so that the mark appears thus: "XXX". Sign your name under the three X's. Do not attempt to study for three more nights. The ability will come to you in a powerful way to override distractions. This is an interesting example of how Sorcery can work. You are *removing the ability* of the distractions to bother you, which strengthens you. If you were to remove the distractions, what would you do the next time and the next time again that more distractions turn up? This Sorcery gives you the power you need.

Base of Skull—To invoke demonic assistance and fortitude.

PROCEDURE—Seek a teacher for this rite or contact me directly. This rite requires multiple punctures and cannot be done without an accomplished mentor.

SORCERY EVENT #5: To Find That Which You Seek

Under Right Breast—If you feel you need guidance in the choices along the path you have already chosen and it is getting complicated.

PROCEDURE—Seek a teacher for this rite or contact me directly for a discussion about this harvesting. It is complicated and may result in a need for sutures.

Right Nipple—If you are absolutely sure of what you seek and need strategy assistance and direction.

PROCEDURE—*Either* have this nipple pierced and obtain the Sacred Elixir through that manner *or* obtain the Sacred Elixir through a solid pin prick. Squeeze the Elixir onto your right index finger and place it beneath your tongue. Sleep and take notice of your dreams. Answers will come in the form of lies. Write them down and do the opposite.

For Females—the Hood (above clitoris) at Center—When what you seek involves an area of life that is of utmost importance and significance, including but not limited to engaging with the disincarnate in significant ways, creating alliances, extraordinarily dark work and for justice.

For Males—Median (nose side) edge of Left Eyebrow— When fighting for a territory and when what you seek involves an area of life that is of utmost importance and significance, including but not limited to engaging with the disincarnate in significant ways, creating alliances, extraordinarily dark work and for justice.

PROCEDURE—You may use the Sacred Elixir obtained this way by writing sigils and notes, and adding to a flame in manners similar to the one listed in the "General Uses" section of the previous chapter. However, there is a second manner in which to use Elixir obtained from these areas. To do that you will have to perform animal sacrifices on small animals (they must fit in the palm of your hand) from land, air and water as well as a lizard or serpent. Their skins will be utilized in a complex rite which I teach to my students. If you have tried all other options and want to pursue this one, you should contact me directly for instruction.

SORCERY EVENT #6: To Cause Death

Under Right Eye—Please seek a teacher for this rite or contact me directly for more information.

PROCEDURE—I suggest you contact a teacher who knows how to do this rite for two reasons: First, because the drawing of the Sacred Elixir from this area is a dangerous procedure, and second, because the procedure itself will work and one must have guidance along the lines of the outcome. As I said earlier, I do not believe in Karma. I do know that when one performs ritual and one experiences a specific outcome, the Sorcerer may have an emotional response which is part of the corporeal experience of the human interaction with the physics of Sorcery. A Sorcerer should be absolutely sure that no other option will produce the desired outcome before considering this procedure.

SORCERY EVENT #7: For Physical Strength

Iliac Crest of Left Pelvis—This event is useful to access your physical strength, your connection to family, ancestry and heritage, as well as to strengthen yourself when physical fortitude is lacking.

PROCEDURE—For seven nights in a row, make small needle punctures and add drops of the Sacred Elixir from this point to red meat. You cannot substitute red meat with anything else here. Eat the meat and rest. The eighth night you will feel tired. From the ninth night on you will gain strength and the sense you desire.

Under Left Mandibular Joint—Plays to your ability or willingness to steady and strengthen yourself to speak freely and trust that which you are saying to be received and useful. Is confidence lacking?

PROCEDURE—Collect the Sacred Elixir carefully with a pinprick as the areas under your jaw are soft tissue and contain nerve bundles and major vessels. Smear it on a mirror. Keep the mirror on the **Altar To Yourself** and add to it in layers of Elixir on top of dried layers (this may take several nights) until you can no longer see through it. When you can no longer see through the Sacred Elixir, place the heart of a strong animal on the mirror so that the animal's Sacred Elixir mixes with your Sacred Elixir. (Even a Turkey heart will do as they are physically strong animals.) Rest your hands on the heart and demand strength. Stay with the heart until you feel the strength you need course through your body. You may feel the heart move as it is picking up an ability to reanimate from the pulse in your palm. Once this is done, wipe the mirror down with the heart, combining as much of the animal and human Sacred Elixir as possible. Collect the heart and place it on the floor of a mausoleum containing the remains of more than three generations of a family known to have wealth and other successes. Wash the mirror and place it in a prominent place so that you will see yourself in it daily. You will grow stronger quickly. Let your ego enjoy the change and help with the momentum.

Left Clavicle—Plays to the question: Are you emotionally involved enough in this work? Are you physically strong enough to combat potential emotional drain? Is Passion and commitment lacking?

PROCEDURE—See the "Demonworks" chapter, Sorcery Event #7

SORCERY EVENT #8: For Mental Strength and to Cope With Stress, and/or to Become Fearless

Top of Left Cheekbones—To cope day to day.

PROCEDURE—Harvest by pinprick and touch the Sacred Elixir on coins each day and spend them. When the amount you spend becomes uncomfortable, your stress will disappear and you will feel less fearful. Reaching that amount faster is up to you.

Lateral edge (ear side) of left cheekbone—To allow for a change of position or attitude.

PROCEDURE—Harvest as above and smear the Sacred Elixir across an image of that which gives you stress. Burn it and wash your hands with the ashes. Sleep and you will wake free from stress.

Point Between Eyebrows—To find solutions to the source problems that caused the stress initially.

PROCEDURE—Seek a teacher for this rite or contact me directly. This process may cause scarring.

Just under front tip of Chin—To develop fearlessness.

PROCEDURE—You will need a larger amount of Sacred Elixir for this Procedure so expect to make a puncture or incision. WARNING—this part of your body is rich with Blood vessels and nerve endings. Please do this ritual with someone you can trust to harvest the Sacred Elixir. Under the tip of chin *does not mean* past the bone. It *does* mean just where the chin turns under and is still in front of the bone line. You will need to collect this Sacred Elixir in vials. Do not refrigerate it. Allow it to putrefy. You will sleep amongst the disincarnate with the vial open and drops from it on your neck, abdomen, ankles, armpits and lips. You must spend the night alone amongst them either on a grave or in a mausoleum. When you wake the next day you will feel distracted and confused. Do not bathe; stay awake and become even more disoriented. Rest where you fall and when you awaken bathe and eat. You have met fearlessness and it is for you to partake.

Men: Top Base of Penis; Women: Base of Coccyx Bone—To choose and strategize confrontation as a method of coping with and solving issues and obtaining Fearlessness.

PROCEDURE—Use in the most comfortable manner as chosen from the "General Uses" section of the previous chapter.

SORCERY EVENT #9: To Create an Impression of Things Being New

Left Armpit Close to Body—This is the only choice for this Sorcery Event.

PROCEDURE—Smear the Sacred Elixir on the inside of some freshly tanned leather and wear it inside your most intimate garment with the Elixir side facing your body. Go to a public event and leave it in an object that is to be thrown away at the end of the event.

SORCERY EVENT #10: To Cause Physical Suffering and Slow Degeneration of an Enemy

Front of right Calf—If you want them to know you are performing this Sorcery.

PROCEDURE—See the "Demonworks" chapter, Sorcery Event #10.

Occiput—If you seek strategy and want to remain anonymous to the Enemy.

PROCEDURE—Work just as in the Demonworks method, but do not deliver the note. Burn it along with the scroll and bury the ash in an infant's grave.

Inside Buttocks close to Anus—If you are hoping for the demise of the individual.

PROCEDURE—Seek a teacher for this rite or contact me directly. Read the Procedure paragraph under Sorcery Event #6.

SORCERY EVENT #11: To Cause Rumors to be Started and Maintained Against a Detractor

Inside of Lower Lip just Right of Center—This is the only choice for this Sorcery Event.

PROCEDURE—Place the Sacred Elixir in blue or purple ink. Using a feather, on onion skin paper, paint the rumor you wish to begin with the soft end of the feather. Burn it and leave the ashes on the property of the detractor. (Property can mean real estate as well as a locker, inside a shoe, etc.)

SORCERY EVENT #12: To Cause Insanity

Any part of Tongue If you want insanity to be the specific area of punishment for the other person; you can cause it to result, for example, by combining this Sorcery event with starting rumors about them at work.

PROCEDURE—This requires contact. Mix your Elixir with pure white sand. Every day for **no fewer than** seven days (must be an odd number), sprinkle the sand on the property of the subject (see property description above). Start with just a tiny bit of sand and increase the amount a bit more each day. By the final day, the amount of sand should be substantial. Only a tiny bit of your Elixir is necessary so the sand should stay mostly white. Do not let anyone else see you do this or know you are doing this. Your detractor will start a downward crumble.

Combined Elixir from BOTH Armpits—These two Elixirs MUST be combined—If you want the sorcery you are doing (such as causing rumors to start about this person) to attach to all areas of their life resulting in insanity.

PROCEDURE—Do as above, then invoke demons by using the 2-sided handprint mentioned in the "Demonworks" chapter, Sorcery Event #10.

SORCERY EVENT #13: To Cure Physical Malady

Elixir of Arches of BOTH feet combined—To cure your own malady.

PROCEDURE—Draw Elixir from the TOP of both arches and then from the BOTTOM of both arches. Combine all four harvestings. Put a combined drop into a glass of red wine and drink it. Do this once on four separate nights. When you are done, find a way to be outside and amongst the disincarnate with your upper body completely naked for no less than three minutes. DEMAND a state of wellness from those disincarnate who can see you. Tell them to plead your case and make an agreement that you will see them and listen to them when you are cured.

Median (navel side) of right Knee

PROCEDURE—Draw the Sacred Elixir and add it to the oil in an oil lamp. Light the lamp in proximity of a place where people die, such as hospitals, hospices, palliative care and geriatric facilities. Sit with the lamp until someone has died and is picked up by an ambulance. This may take a while but curing a physical malady is the type of Sacred Elixir Sorcery that involves making deals with the disincarnate. When a body is brought out demand from the newly disincarnate that they "destabilize time and my illness." When you feel an event such as an unexplained wind or touch or sound, immediately put the flame out and leave the lamp sitting on the ground. Walk away and do not turn back.

Combined four points between Chin Tip and Left Mandibular Joint—To cure another's maladies (when that person is not available to provide their own Elixir for your use on their behalf).

PROCEDURE—Seek a teacher for this rite or contact me directly. The blood must be drawn in a particular way that may cause scarring if done inappropriately.

SORCERY EVENT #14: To Access Attending Demons

Over Heart—Deep Scratch left to drip and dry on chest, shows willingness.

PROCEDURE—See the "Demonworks" chapter Sorcery Event #14. Additional comment: Attending Demons do not come so readily to those who cannot yet command them. Occasionally they will come to the individual to give notice that they cannot yet stay.

SORCERY EVENT #15: To Draw Scrying Elixir

Under the Tongue Both Sides—This is the absolute second best location (aside from one other which I will only share with my students due to the danger of harvesting the Elixir from that unmentioned spot).

PROCEDURE—See the "Scrying" chapter.

SORCERY EVENT #16: To Force Affection and Gifts

Both Wrists combined; palm side, mixed with genital Sacred Elixir—This can be used to force any kind of affection, and can be extraordinarily powerful when used to get someone to leave you everything in their wills. There are many types of affection……

Allow me to first say that using Sorcery to take someone from an existing partner is vulgar and inappropriate. Why, you may ask, would I make such a statement here and not in areas of Sorcery that deal with life and death? Well, we all have areas of the human experience that we view with contempt and I view the manipulation of partnerships through Sorcery as contemptible as it often results in the Sorcerer not getting what they thought they would get in the affected person. I also know that there are plenty amongst you that will do it anyway and that isn't mine to worry about. There is a huge chasm between using Sorcery to open one's 'eyes,' allowing them to see potential partners and helping someone who seeks love to find room in their life to accept it—versus deciding someone should be your partner and taking them through Sorcery. The act of doing so seems to change the fiber of the person who is being moved. What is delivered is a sort of emotional zombie (in the social, not the literal sense). It is as if this particular kind of Sorcery changes them in a profound way. It is much like raising the dead as the person you will obtain will not be as you recall them. Something comes back, but they will not be who they were.

PROCEDURE—Mix the Sacred Elixirs together in a blue glass dish or on a glass tile. Add to it a biological of the intended. If you cannot get a biological, use handwriting or an image. Using blue ink, write your desires on a tiny piece of organic material such as a leaf or animal parchment. Cut the materials small enough to be able to grind them together with the Elixir using a pestle. Place the mixture on the positive drawing (attraction) side of a magnet. Allow the mixture to dry on the magnet. Using a slaughtered fowl intended as food, place the magnet deep in the throat of the fowl approaching from the opened chest and moving upward. Bury the beast with its head facing north on hallowed ground or in a cemetery of any kind. Bury it deep, no less than two feet. Sleep overnight on the spot with your head facing exactly the same way as the head of the buried fowl. At sunup, stand up and make sure your physical impression is noticeable in the ground. Turn away from the place and walk away. Stay awake and shower at sunset. Results will become evident.

SORCERY EVENT #17: To Remove Sorcery Done Upon Someone/Self

Center Throat, both inner Wrists, under Tongue, Top of Both Feet—Done with the victim's Elixir and their CONSENT; although I discuss non-Consensual collection of Elixir later in this book, using only consensually collected Elixir for this particular Sorcery Event will cause an effective outcome. NOTE: **the throat and neck and the wrists are filled with Arteries and Veins of extraordinary significance.** *Extreme caution is advised.*

PROCEDURE—Seek a teacher for this rite or contact me directly.

SORCERY EVENT #18: To Freeze a Tongue that has Spoken Against You

Back of Left Knee—If you want the person to simply stop.

PROCEDURE—Make an incision and wipe up the Sacred Elixir directly from the incision with a photo, handwriting or combination thereof, and/or a biological of the person who has spoken against you. It is vital that there is *no step* between cutting and placing the materials upon the incision. Place the materials inside a split mammal tongue or liver, or the gills of a large fish. (Note: Use only the organs/sections, not the entire animal). Place the organ on hot coals with the thinnest surface of the "meat" covering the added items directly onto the coals. For example, if you are using a fish, place the materials inside the slit open gills and set them with skin side down against the coals. As the burning begins, spit on the materials with as much saliva as you can garner. Spit a total of seventeen times over the next few minutes. They will lose the ability to continue speaking of you in this manner.

Under right nipple—If you want the person to stop and feel the same effects of the damage you have experienced from their deeds.

(Never mix these two Elixirs)

PROCEDURE—Do as above and continue as follows: After the burning is done, collect some of the ashes and charred remains. Grind them and roll them in cigarette paper. Coat the "cigarette" with an accelerant such as lighter fluid or gasoline. Gather sand into a metal container, preferably a silver pot, and add to it something from the home or grounds of the intended person. Place the pot somewhere they could see from their home (it does not matter if they actually see it—it only matters that it is within sight lines). Light the tip of a long piece of twig or stick that has been on their property and light the "cigarette" from that flame. When it goes out they will begin to feel the effects of their actions.

SORCERY EVENT #19: To Cause Fertility (Consensual)

(Use the Elixir of the woman who is desirous of conception)

Clitoral (that is the most powerful and most painful to harvest)—If it is believed the reason for difficulty in conception is physical.

Fertility work is an oddly grey area of my work as it begs the question of manipulation of the disincarnate—if you believe in souls or reincarnation. If one is summoning birth and you have those beliefs, then you may feel that one is cheating or repelling Death. This is why I feel strongly that beliefs in gods of any kind are anathema to Sorcery work. Please form your own cognitive contents as they pertain to calling back "souls" or beings that have passed. There is a section about this in the "Corporeal Necromancy" chapter as it pertains to bringing the disincarnate back via reintroduction of the individual through a newly formed human. However, that area addresses an agreement to bring a specific individual back into living form.

PROCEDURE—Draw the Sacred Elixir with a syringe or ask a phlebotomist to do so for you. Place it into three small vials, one of which is red. I have found that a solution for obtaining colored vials is to use clear vials and paint them on the outside with nail polish. One coat usually leaves a semi-transparent effect and this allows for any combination of glass vials needed. Obtain three new bricks.

There are many options here in the work of fertility, so I will present the one with which I have had the best results. You will need an article from a deceased infant (any child who has not reached their first birthday). This is not easy to come by so I suggest you prowl funeral homes and, at very least, obtain a wake card, stop at the casket and touch it to the body. (As obtaining the human artifacts needed for this work is difficult, it is helpful to develop associations with those who work in funeral homes and morgues.) Place the article around or under the red vial. Next, gather soil from a freshly dug infant grave (simple to find at any large cemetery; freshly dug means that the soil still has an appearance of being recently moved and is not truly settled), and make a packet by wrapping it in fabric that contains body fluids from sexual contact between the intended parents. (If the woman is attempting to conceive via a sperm-donor process, then she will need to collect sperm during that procedure and wipe it on her undergarments and use that fabric.) Place the second vial into this packet.

Obtain a powerful rare earth magnet. Wrap it in plastic and place it inside the vaginal opening and sleep one whole hour with it as such. Remove it and place the third vial of the Sacred Elixir upon it, checking for polarity so that the positive side is touching the vial. Place the three bricks standing vertically so that the longest sides touch and form a platform. Place all three tableaus on the small brick altar with the magnet one in the middle so that they touch one another. Continue on with the process of conception via sexual activity or artificial means. Within the month conception will occur. Once conception is complete, bury all three items in the grave from which you gathered the soil (with the tops of the vials opened for the first time since collecting the Sacred Elixir), and throw the bricks into moving water such as a river or ocean.

Right Armpit (where it Joins the Body)—To create fertility when the woman is not ovulating to meet the time constraint needs of a particular event.

PROCEDURE—Do all as above and *add* the Elixir from the Right Armpit by smearing it on the magnet.

Inside Navel (Difficult to extract)—If you believe the reasons for difficulty in conception is other than physical, or if you believe someone has done Sorcery to prevent fertility.

PROCEDURE—Do all as is above, *but first add* the Elixir from inside the Navel to red wine. Take a mouthful and spit it onto the bricks *prior* to placing the three tableaus upon them.

SORCERY EVENT #20: To Cause Fertility (Non-Consensual), such as to cause someone to conceive against their will.

(Use the Elixir of a woman who has had at least one living child, NOT the elixir of the intended victim)

Clitoral (that is the most powerful yet painful to harvest)— If you believe the woman is using contraception or is physically incapable.

Right Armpit where it joins the Body—If you believe the woman is completely capable of becoming pregnant and you want to speed up the process.

Inside Navel (difficult to extract)—If you believe the woman has Protection Sorcery on her and you want to get around it.

PROCEDURE—DO ALL EXACTLY THE SAME AS ABOVE with the Sacred Elixir from a woman who has had at least one living child and is NOT the person for whom this Sorcery Event is meant. It is especially helpful if the donor is a person related to the person who has an interest in having conception occur. People have many reasons for performing this Sorcery. Occasionally someone will do it to try to prevent a couple from splitting, to create an heir, etc. The purpose of the work is personal and not a cause for my concern.

SORCERY EVENT #21: To Cause Infertility

If a man or a woman comes to you asking to make them infertile (there are many reasons one may do this), then use their own Sacred Elixir. If you are working on someone who has not asked you to do this, use the Elixir of a woman who is no longer fertile. (There is one other type of elixir that can be used here but I will only share this information with my students.)

Top side of Both Thighs Mixed with either Semen or Tears—The thigh Sacred Elixir must be FEMALE so if you are a male you must acquire it from a WILLING female.

PROCEDURE—Collect the Sacred Elixir and the semen or tears. Place them in a black glass vial and add three drops of water in which bitter herbs have soaked for three days, *or* three drops of a strongly bitter liqueur such as Campari. Shake the contents every hour for twenty-four hours. Pour the mixture into the bladder of an animal (sheep or cow is preferable but you may also use the bladder of a small animal of any kind). The GENDER of the animal MUST MATCH the gender of the intended. Hammer three nails into the bladder. Bury the bladder in the grave of someone you believe died childless. Carry a magnet with the negative polarity facing outward on your left side for fourteen days and nights. The intended will not conceive or cause conception. There is a way to reverse this; please contact me if you need to do so.

SORCERY EVENT #22: To Cause Dementia

Under Tongue—If you want the Dementia to be slow in coming, causing the person to slowly lose their footing in society.

Under Lower Eyelid—For rapid-onset dementia.

Top of Both Inner Thighs close to Genitals—to cause addictive behaviors and/or inappropriate actions to be demonstrated by the victim, resulting in psychiatric detainment and humiliation.

PROCEDURE—Seek a teacher for this rite or contact me directly, as it is very possible to turn the results upon yourself without careful guidance.

SORCERY EVENT #23: To Cause Blindness

(Must use *victim's* Sacred Elixir. There is no other option.)

Right Knee inside where it would touch the left knee if legs were together. Must be liquid (not on a bandage).

PROCEDURE—Seek a teacher for this Sorcery Event or contact me directly, as it is very possible to turn the results upon yourself without careful guidance.

SORCERY EVENT #24: To Inhibit Someone's Ability to Communicate

Left Palm—Immediate and temporary results.

PROCEDURE—Use a photograph or a sketch of the intended and place it face up on a surface that will be undisturbed. Make an incision inside your left palm, and, without touching the Elixir with anything else including your fingers, place the incision over the mouth in the photograph and press down hard using a small and tight pivoting, smothering motion. Do this until you feel a sense of silence and peace. Leave the photo for at least three nights, rip it up and discard it in the open such as throwing the pieces around in a park. This should last for at least a few weeks. If need be, do it again.

Wrist (outer, pinky side)—Long-term results.

PROCEDURE—Do as above; however after three nights burn the photo. Bring the ashes as close to the intended as possible and make every effort to get the ash onto the intended. One way is to put it on their chair at work. Make sure they are the first one to sit in it once the ash is placed there.

Ring Finger—To inhibit someone's ability to communicate with a specific person or with yourself.

PROCEDURE—Do all as above; however, the ash **must** be ingested by the intended. I suggest you put it in some dark beverage. They only need to ingest a small amount for the Sorcery Event to be effective. The outcome will be permanent and the person may lose their ability to communicate altogether, depending on how many people have expressed disdain for them.

SORCERY EVENT #25: To Cause Someone to be Thought of as a Fool

Sublingual (under tongue) mixed with Sacred Elixir from between big and next toes (either foot)—This will cause short term results. To make the results long term or specific to ONE person in particular thinking the victim is a fool, add Ring Finger Elixir. This Sorcery Event can also be performed by placing items in the bed of the targeted person. Inquire privately to me about that method.

PROCEDURE—Mix the Sacred Elixir with ink and steal a piece of reading matter from the intended. Even a newspaper will work, but best results come from a book the intended has carried around and to which they have developed a sense of attachment. A bible or religious book is my favorite object for this Sorcery Event.

Tear out a page, return the item to them without their knowledge, and using your Elixir ink, draw a stick figure of the person and write their name *across* the stick figure as if in a child's handwriting. Nail it to a tree in a pet cemetery, or somewhere near where animals are buried or slaughtered, well above eye level. Leave it there until it rots away. As the image degrades so will the ability for your detractor to be taken seriously by their peers.

SORCERY EVENT #26: To Gain Wealth

Harvest three Vials of Elixir; two from the center point between the Navel and Base of Penis *or* Top of Pubic Mound, *and* one from your left palm

PROCEDURE—This is a fairly simple rite. Place the three vials on a metal surface. Mix salt into one vial, honey into another and either semen, breast milk, placenta or menstrual Sacred Elixir into the third. Set them together in a triangle so they are all touching one another. Point the positive polarity side of three magnetic rods toward them. Create a puncture wound in your left palm and drip the Sacred Elixir onto the positive points of the rods and into the center where the three bottles meet. Using your left middle finger, dip into the Elixir on your palm and anoint your throat and bottoms of your feet. Stay still and quiet until you start to hear metallic clicking sounds. At that point walk away from the vials and do not revisit them for several hours. The next sundown thrust the rods into the earth at the gravesite of someone of wealth in the following steps:

- Positive side into the earth at the head level
- Negative side into the earth at the heart level
- Positive side into the earth at the foot level
- Take soil from this grave and bring it to the next one:
- Find a pauper's grave and sprinkle one half of the grave dirt upon it; then bury the three vials open and upright in the pauper's grave as follows:
- The vial with salt at the feet
- The vial with honey at the heart
- The vial with the biological at the head

Say "Corrections have been made." Walk away and shower. Wealth will present itself.

SORCERY EVENT #27: To Gain Health (Physical)

Balls of Both Feet mixed

PROCEDURE—See the "Demonworks" chapter, Sorcery Event #27.

SORCERY EVENT #28: Protection Against Physical Attack that will Render all Attackers Physically Impaired

Under both breasts mixed with Left Inner Forearm—There is only one formula for this that is effective one hundred percent of the time. Make sure you mix equal quantities.

PROCEDURE—I will not specify the quantity of Sacred Elixir here, as this is one of the few times that quantity is important, and the amount you need to gather is significant. You will need an assistant to gather this much. Seek a teacher for this rite or contact me directly.

SORCERY EVENT #29: Protection Against Non-Physical Attacks that will Cause Dementia in the Attackers

Both Clavicles mixed—There is only one option for this Sorcery Event.

PROCEDURE—I will not specify the quantity of Sacred Elixir here, as this is one of the few times that quantity is important, and the amount you need to gather is significant. You will need an assistant to gather this much. Seek a teacher for this rite or contact me directly.

SORCERY EVENT #30: To Make a Man Give You His Property to Keep or Borrow

(Excellent for obtaining a House or Apartment)

Cut or scratch this symbol into the flattest area just above your genitals:

PROCEDURE—Use a business card or something similar from the owner. Turn it upside down and tape it on top of the cut area with the writing on the card touching the Sacred Elixir. Wear it for at least seventy hours; do not bathe during this time. The home or items will be yours. Dispose of the card in a graveyard after you obtain the item or move in.

CONSUMPTION:
THE SEX OF BLOOD SORCERY

Blood Sorcery has significant applications when applied to sex, and is able to even further utilize sexual energy by exploiting the benefits of orgasm and pulse rate into the Sacred Elixir, thereby giving it additional strength. As in all things Sorcery-related, there are consensual and non-consensual rituals. Sorcerers are by nature predatory; therefore the joining of sex and the harvesting of and usage of the Sacred Elixir are perfect matches with an enhanced outcome. On the subject of how Sorcery is received, my good friend Mr. Rouge said:

> "Sorcery requires no dogma but free will, no prophet, no pope, no ayatollah. If there is one qualifier that can universally be applied to sorcery it is "unfathomable." When magicians stare into the abyss, they have to be surrounded by talismans and protective spells; when sorcerers do so, the most we have to worry about is the rules of etiquette, because we dwell in the ancient and complex realms where the others lie."
>
> — *Mr. Rouge, June, 2011*

When discussing sex as it can be used as a Blood Sorcery ritual, the first question that comes to mind is, "What's to be gained?" The answer is not a simple one. I have discovered that sex can be used as an additional facet to most rituals, but particular to Blood Sorcery, harvesting of the Sacred Elixir during or just before or after orgasm offers a way to access Blood that has been in your body during an activity of hormone rush and increased pulse rate. This imbues the Sacred Elixir with a sense-memory of desperation, desire and the goal of pleasure and orgasm. Elixir collected under these circumstances is doubly sacred to the Sorceress who harvests it as it represents the same goals of desire and satisfaction. Therefore, the collector and the collected are of a unique and singular mind in the search for an attainment of pleasure.

If you are completely prepared to do a ritual and cut, puncture or slash your lover or yourself during orgasm and bring that Blood directly to the ritual without losing much time, you are working with a heightened Elixir and a powerful catalyst. It will also change and elevate the fiber of who you are as a Sorcerer and make for extraordinary attachments to sex and sorcery. I have done this enough times to know that the performance of the harvested Elixir is like no other, and the performance of the Sorceress is elevated.

Another usage of sex in Blood Sorcery requires that your lover also be involved in the sorcery at hand. Harvesting each other's Sacred Elixir during sex and combining it to create an Elixir that has had the benefit of the orgasms of multiple individuals—as well as the benefit of the combined energy of lovers—is a magnificent product to use if you are both of like mind about the desired outcome.

Consider slashing each other during orgasm, sucking out the Blood and spitting it into a glass. That combined Elixir could be flaked on glass and added to ink for the writing element of sorcery to enhance passions. Saliva has very little DNA as compared to other biologicals so it is less likely to contaminate the Sacred Elixir.

Semen and Blood mixed together make an extraordinary biological potion whether semen is mixed with the Blood of a man or a woman. Consider making agreements with partners to facilitate these contributions. This is the Sex of Sorcery so do not become overly concerned about relationship and love and the things of romance here. We are discussing the collection of biologicals through the primal actions of sex and orgasm—simple combinations, simple equations. If there is a male and a female in the equation, the combined Elixir is more varied and stronger, offering a tremendous contribution.

The potion formed will be of significant variation resulting in increased strength when created from individuals with no shared ancestry. Both lover's Sacred Elixir combined with semen will create a potion-like Elixir, useful for the Sorcery of fertility, the obtaining of land by purchase or duplicity, revenge and justice, and the intentional perpetration of illness both physical and mental.

Unquestionably, the most powerful brew that can be created is done in the following way and requires a man and a menstruating woman:

- Both individuals should harvest Sacred Elixir from their chests, cutting as close to the pulsing heart as possible. Make this a shallow cut as to not injure the chest wall.
- Using the middle and ring fingers of his left hand, he collects his chest blood directly from the wound and pushes it deeply into her vaginal opening; as she then clamps her vaginal muscles as tightly as possible as if attempting to stop him from removing his fingers.
- Using the middle and ring fingers of her right hand, she collects his chest blood directly from the wound and coats the head of his penis with the Sacred Elixir on her fingers.
- Neither participant should clean the Blood from their hands.
- The couple now has vaginal sex and he ejaculates inside of her.
- When they are done, using her left hand she gathers as much as possible of the potion inside of her and that which lingers on him, joining them together onto a piece of glass and allowing them to dry.

- The mixture is flaked and stored in glass vials worn by the couple and added occasionally to rituals by reanimating the flakes in fresh blood either in ink or vodka.
- The flakes are used in sorcery of gain and destruction and death. This is *not* a fertility ritual.

This is a powerful ritual and has nothing to do with love. Gay couples should consider performing this ritual with close sorcery associates in order to obtain this unstoppable 'potion'. This act can also be used as a marriage of Blood Sorcerers. Sex isn't love, it's sex, and in this situation it yields powerful benefits.

Masturbation

The same principles apply to obtaining Sacred Elixir that has been privy to the pulse increase and hormones of sex during masturbation. Before you begin create the incision by whichever method you prefer. The increased heart rate will cause the bleeding to increase and you will get the Elixir you desire. Use Blood that has been through this experience immediately. There is no point to harvesting this kind of Elixir and storing it. It will not retain the power it garnered through orgasm for long and will return to the state of Sacred Elixir harvested under ordinary circumstances.

Erotic Harvesting of the Sacred Elixir by Additional Methods

Harvesting the Elixir for another or having another harvest it for you during an intimate act produces an enriched Sacred Elixir as well. Piercings and tattoos and other body modifications fall into this category. Blood from these events is powerful as it has the rare component of chosen pain. An example of taking this one step further is in the event of, for example, a scrotum piercing and combining this powerful residual Blood from the piercing with semen produced during, before or after the actual piercing. Piercings such as this are often done during an erection and it is not uncommon for the person receiving the piercing to find the experience erotic as well. The mixture of Blood and Semen is always a powerful potion. Flake it and add it to ink and use it for the sorcery of taking opportunity and forcing outcomes, taking that which you desire away from another, being released from confinement, taking a house away from its owner, and tipping the odds that you will be chosen for anything from an adoption to a Grammy. This is Sorcery, boundless and dogma free.

77% COMMITMENT

STUDENT QUESTION: Why isn't my sorcery working?

It is a matter of commitment. *Everything* is a matter of commitment. One needs to look at one's whole life and be candid and self-interviewing. If you had hired yourself as a life manager would you fire yourself or give yourself a raise? One has to take inventory and ask oneself what is and is not working. If you are brutally honest with yourself, you will find many things that are extraneous or contrary to the work of Sorcery. I have a number in mind, this percentage of perceived commitment, and the number is seventy-seven percent.

That is the percentage I believe people genuinely commit to projects, choices, relationships, etc., and Sorcery is no exception. People feel satisfied with their commitment at seventy-seven percent and they begin to convince themselves that they are completely committed. They have enlisted more than three quarters of the way and they believe this is what it feels like when they are expressing commitment, but that is not the case.

I CAN TELL YOU WHAT IT FEELS LIKE TO BE 100%
COMMITTED, AS THAT IS A VERY SIMPLE
DESCRIPTION. IT FEELS LIKE IT LOOKS, LIKE
WINNING, & HAVING, & ENJOYING YOUR POWER.

There are events in life that just do not fit the criteria of having a viable point of no return because they exist in their entirety from the onset. A woman can be at the beginning of a pregnancy, yet in reality she is no less pregnant than she will be at month nine. We allow ourselves the escape route of pretending that becoming more **developed** at something is the same as **more** of something. It is not. At nine months the child she carries is bigger, more people know she is pregnant, it is now not possible to do things she could do six months ago—but she was one hundred percent pregnant at the beginning and she is one hundred percent pregnant at nine months.

Regarding the experience of observing and noting reactions, most people approach commitments a way out already figured into the equation. I refer to this as an excuse and an escape. **That approach is a guaranteed path to failure**. As much as it may appear to allow for choices, it does not. All it allows for is **failure**.

Even having a "backup plan" is a sure way to guarantee that you will not achieve your primary goal in its greatest form. Backup plans are a strategy of cowardice and evidence of a dress rehearsal mentality. Approaches like these do not force one to have to edit oneself or develop the important skill of finding a way to function at top potential while feeling or being confined. It **does** allow for lowering the bar and finding even greater ways of failing to complete the task rather than fulfilling the goal. One should take on a commitment that forces self-editing and may even force one to have to say "no" to oneself on occasion. Saying "no" is not denying oneself anything—it is a method of taking inventory and deciding what is and is not necessary.

This is harder for some than others: the weak will find that during those moments of learning to say "no" to themselves, they will feel uncomfortable and perhaps lost. The weakest of the weak will mistake this discomfort as a sign that they are "outside of their comfort zone" and "stretching their abilities" while the truth is that they are simply uncomfortable. **If ANYTHING in this section reminds you of the way you are currently proceeding, then that is why your Sorcery isn't working.**

I am offering these words at this point because this is how Sorcerers live. As those who have listened to my radio show know, I live my life of Blood Sorcery out in the open. Fearlessly I teach, discuss, and communicate via many types of media exchanges and am certainly not in the closet about what I do. The first time I said on the radio **"Sacred Elixir"** with specific regard to Blood and Blood Sorcery, I was amazed at the amount of correspondence I received. Much of it was from those who feel the term is exclusive to the Catholic usage of the wine at mass, and others wrote joyfully that they felt there was honor in referring to their own Blood in this way. Some felt I was taking a chance with my safety by declaring that we **all** possess Sacred Elixir in our bodies, but I live my sorcery life the same way I live the rest of my life. I invest one hundred percent into anything I am doing and cannot allow fear to guide me.

THE TRUTH OF THE THING IS THAT IF ONE CANNOT BRING A 100% COMMITMENT TO SOMETHING, ONE CANNOT EXPECT A 100% RETURN ON THAT INVESTMENT.

Sorcery is a black and white example of how commitment works. Sorcery is **results-based** or it is non-existent. If it doesn't produce the effects—the outcome that you desire—then it was not done correctly or you are not taking the position of a one hundred percent participant. Sorcery demands tangible results. Make sure you are doing everything you can and making every change needed to get those results.

Could It Be That Simple?

Sorcery is the participation in and the manipulation of physics from the inside, allowing yourself to prove to yourself on an ongoing basis that you are part of the equation. Using energy (and I do not mean "energy" in the New Age sense of the term) as if it is electricity directly out of the socket is the most direct way to work. **Blood Sorcery is, in my opinion, the purest and strongest method of Sorcery to create direct hits**—and to use those hits to make absolute changes or redirect energy from one issue or person to the intended target. **Blood Sorcery is the only absolute sorcery with no need for external tools.**

THE ONLY ELIXIR WE WILL EVER NEED FLOWS WITHIN US AND WE ARE ALREADY PART OF ITS MAGNIFICENT MAGNETIC EQUATION.

Take, for example, the following scenario:

A position becomes available that you want and you discover your best friend is up for it as well. Remembering that Sorcery is not for the timid, the green girl, or the karma-trapped type, do you use sorcery to get the position? If you are not willing to use sorcery to get it then you are not fully committed to Sorcery—you are, at most, seventy-seven percent.

If that sounds uncomfortable or cold, think of it this way:

Understand that if you say you are willing to use **all of your talents, skills and references** to compete for that job—against your friend or anyone else who is in line for the position—then Sorcery should not be excluded from your arsenal. If you are not using your ability to perform Sorcery Events, then you are full of nonsense and self-medicating lies because **one of your skills is Sorcery** and it is there to be used just like any other skill that may get you that job. If you don't use it, then you are not sincere and you are not a Sorcerer. If you were a member of a religion that hands all of its major life results over to a divinity, you would pray. In the true act of prayer, one is asking for an intervening effort from a more powerful source. This has an effect on the one praying as it gives them a sense of practical application of using all that is in their arsenal. That is **their** Sorcery. Why are you not using **your** Sorcery?

If you cannot say that you are willing to use sorcery to get the job then you are not a Sorceress. If you have a belief that Sorcery is lingering on your list of extraneous skills, and not an immediate part of your internal response pattern, then you do not yet understand that effective Sorcery cannot be something performed now and then and at best you are seventy-seven percent—but you are not a Sorcerer.

Final Words on Commitment

You cannot put seventy-seven percent into your marriage, relationships, parenting, work, passions, pets, etc., if you desire a one hundred percent return on the outcome of those endeavors. You cannot expect to get a dollar for seventy-seven cents and you cannot expect to get one hundred percent of the results with a seventy-seven percent commitment. If what you want from the experiences of Blood Sorcery is a one hundred percent outcome, you have to put in a one hundred percent commitment.

COMFORT IN THE DARKNESS

We, Blood Sorcerers and Necromancers, tend not to be people of the sun.

We are death workers, funeral directors, morgue workers, night people. We do not decorate our homes with sunflowers and pots full of plants requiring sunlight, sheer curtains and wall-to-wall tan carpets. **Get in front of the mirror of admittance** on this one readers. You know the truth. You are who you are in this or you are not.

We don't live in sunny places. We don't live among bright beach cultures; we walk the beach only at night enjoying its sterile air and the cool agreement sand makes with tide. We accept relationships with the disincarnate to get our work done. The disincarnate are light-sensitive and because of our associations to them, so are we. Why pretend otherwise?

If you want your sorcery to work, you must approach your sorcery with one hundred percent commitment and embrace that you are willing to reach inside your arterial structures and withdraw opportunity in the presence of a band-aid society. That is not the stuff of current culture or casual living.

You cannot run both with the fox and with the hounds; it must be one or the other.

THE DANGER OF "BELIEF CLUTTER" AND APOLOGIES

If in your home you are surrounded by the baptism crucifix your family gave to you when you were put through, against your will and as in infant without your ability to give consent, a religious rite of enormous importance to that particular sect, then you have Belief Clutter. Sentimental attachments to the white dress you wore at your "first holy communion" at age seven when they married you off to god, creates an entrapment of things forced upon you when you were in possession of an **infant's or child's mind**. It is irrelevant to me if you believe in these things or not. My purpose here is to tell you that **you cannot serve two masters and as Sorcerers you should not serve *any* masters**. If you are to be a Blood Sorcerer and you continue to live amongst this Belief Clutter while you are in possession of an adult mind and know full well that these antiquated beliefs no longer fit your life, then you are living in a fragmented physical reality that will damage or significantly halt your progress.

Imagine you are newly married and in your home you are keeping photos of your ex-spouse and sleeping on the bed from a previous marriage. The items themselves hold no power. The power is in the visceral response to those items by you and your new spouse. If you throw the items away no one will punish you—there is no photo frame or mattress god judging you here. Throw away the crucifix; no one will strike you dead. The question becomes "**Can** you do it, and if not, why not?" Are you still attached to the guilt or fragments of a belief system that no longer serves you?

Either way, you have a master and Sorcery requires us to be our own master.

For example, when you invoke your own immensely personal and powerful Sorcery under the bleeding crucifix from your first communion, the question of the meaning of blood and your right to use your own as you see fit is tainted from all your primary school days when you were controlled by the nonsense of catechism. Self-doubt becomes empowered by the presence of these religious artifacts just as the bed from the first marriage would fuel relationship doubt.

I wrote a little book once called *Spiritual Virginity: 31 Days to a Personal Spiritual Exorcism Using Your Adult Mind.* The book offers the reader thirty-one days and nights of work to remove the remnants of previous belief systems from their lives. A simplified nightly lighting of a black candle and a white candle, symbolically balance the energy within you and allow you to start from an even plane, letting go of the beliefs put upon you when you possessed only a child's mind, and allowing yourself a way to see and judge these beliefs with your adult mind. There are other tasks to do and things to say to reprogram the participant to a plane of **no** beliefs, and allow the choosing of beliefs. It was not a perfect book and the color of candles means nothing. Yet I chose Black and White as both a psychological catalyst and a metaphor to emphasize that one must choose one's beliefs from a blank place, without the taint of those beliefs that were chosen for you; and that one cannot serve two masters.

Belief Clutter is deadly to the practice of Sorcery. If you are still carrying bits of decomposed beliefs and you feel uncomfortable that you have neglected these beliefs, or you feel guilt that you no longer accept these beliefs, **then you are living in a room full of fractured emotions and expired contracts and you cannot clear your mind for Sorcery.**

Adults **should** be making difficult decisions. The action of choices on this level is what separates our child minds from our adult minds.

> **SORCERY IS A SELFISH ACT. IT IS A BRILLIANT ACT, A POWERFUL ACT AND IT IS AN ACT THAT WILL ABSOLUTELY GET YOU WHAT YOU WANT WHEN PROPERLY EXECUTED WITH SKILL AND 100% COMMITMENT.**

No Apologies

The need to constantly apologize raises many of the same issues as the distraction of Belief Clutter. **Extraneous apologies are tiny fractures in your acceptance of yourself as a member of the experience called Sorcery.** Do not apologize for practicing Blood Sorcery. If you do, then the very act of Sorcery is compromised.

I want to tell this brief story. Recently I was asked to teach a class in a suburban area and show some of my animal mummies. I was told by the organizers that they would **have to** use my first name and that they would **not be** using **Sorceress,** the title I use all the time. I told them that was completely unacceptable. They argued that their clientele **found the word "Sorceress" to be scary.** So the participants were willing to take a class on making talismans made with their own Blood and throw a reception for mummified animals...but the word **Sorceress** was too scary. I didn't apologize by letting them make this adjustment, I simply cancelled the class, and denied them my presence and the presence of my mummies. Get ready to be expected to apologize if Sorcery is your path.

The big question remains: Just what are you apologizing for? Break down your reflex on choosing to apologize. Are you apologizing for practicing something different than that which is the belief of your parents and neighbors? Are you apologizing for feeling that you are fringe, unconventional, dangerous, for being perceived to be an embarrassment? Perhaps you are apologizing for failing "them" in their expectations of you. You will have to stop apologizing if you expect to perform Sorcery, because those who feel an apology is owed will disappear from your life eventually anyway as you grow in your practice.

REVEALING YOURSELF

There is a vast chasm between making a public statement—such as having a radio show and telling the world you are a Blood Sorcerer—and actively denying that you are one. You don't have to put a public face on it as I do. That being said, denial is toxic to the work of Sorcery. A student asked me what happens if I deny that I am Sorceress? To whom are you denying it? When someone asks if you are a practitioner of Sorcery and you say no, because the act of Sorcery is energy, the energy itself is impacted by "hearing" you denounce participation with it. Such a denial will affect the flow of energy into any relationship between yourself and Sorcery. Sorcery cannot actually hear you—you hear yourself and this denial chips away at your commitment. Denial is a powerful breech in energy; therefore, denial is one additional impediment to one's ability to have one hundred percent outcomes in sorcery.

It is very much like denying a personal relationship. If you deny that you are romantically involved with someone when you are, in fact, lovers, just imagine how that denial impacts the person whom you are denying. Sorcery—through the energy of sorcery and all things being physics—experiences denial the same way, not from the outside but from an internal bit of your personal denial, and pulls away its own commitment to you as the practitioner.

> **SORCERY REQUIRES A SELFISH PURITY TO THE TRUTH OF YOUR PRACTICE.**

93

The main personal requirement to successful Sorcery (other than skills and knowledge), is to discard the remnants of beliefs and half-truths hanging off the side and pulling energy away from your practice of Sorcery. There are no weak or cluttered Sorcerers, but there are many weak and cluttered students of Sorcery. To move from student to Sorcerer the student must remove both Belief Clutter and the need to apologize as part of the training.

Sorcery has no grey areas. You cannot effect a partial change if you are using sorcery for a specific event. If the sorcery you are doing is to obtain a house that five other people have bids on—you can't obtain it a little bit—you can't "sort of" obtain it—you get the house or you don't, no grey area. Get in all the way. That is how it has to be with Sorcery.

FULL PARTICIPATION YIELDS FULL OUTCOME.

So what other cracks in your Sorcery are causing it not to work? You must not be timid or vague; Sorcery requires one hundred percent clarity and an ability to be demanding. Successful Sorcery must be approached from a position that you already have that which you seek—it already exists, and Sorcery is your map to find it. It is the oldest principle of Sorcery and is spoken of in ancient grimoires, key systems, etc. It should be no surprise that the idea has been hijacked by new age gurus who ask you to pair it with white light and gratitude journals. That is a combination that allows only partial fulfillment and creates just enough gain to attach the reader of new age visualization games to their gurus, selling more gear and books and wish cards.

EXPECTING, TRYING, HOPING, WISHING, PRAYING AND PATIENCE—ARE ALL TERMS OF *ANTICIPATION* AND NOT TERMS OF *COMPLETION*—KEEPING YOU CAPTIVE IN THE PLACE OF NOT YET HAVING, CREATING AN UNFORTUNATE NEED FOR GURUS.

I do not wish to be anyone's guru. I teach what I know to those who want to learn, and then use it as they see fit.

I will tell you this: you are not going to be in the place of "having it" if you use the language of *process and desire*. To **have it** you will already have to **be in the place of having it** and Sorcery is the compass to locating it. Use the compass to locate what which you require and then accept it as yours even though you don't yet see the item it in your home.

When I stand in the portal and I am about to make something happen, my Blood Sorcery is only an acknowledgement that it has already happened, that I have already received the outcome which I desire. When I step up and use the materials of my Sacred Elixir and magnets, I have received the call stating **that which I desire is already here,** that I already have it, already know it and have already received it. Sorcery brings it to my doorstep. Here is the enormous commitment that I have, that I am in complete acceptance and have already received my desired outcome even if that outcome is unusually dark.

Sorcery is not about deserving; it is about serving the desire to have. The issue of self-deserving is something to work out way before you step up to Sorcery. As Sorcerers we must remember that it is vital to demand that which we desire.

Action

**100% action + 100% knowing + 100% involvement =
Sorcery hitting the mark**

Take away as many variables as you can. That's a good strategy no matter what you are planning in your life. If you are in complete acceptance that you have the perfect amount of skills, understand the material, and have accrued all the knowledge you can gather, then you are ready to perform Sorcery Events. If you don't have all the information, then you are simply not ready. There is only one way to find out how strong your skills already are: *perform some Sorcery*. It is perfectly acceptable to start small, experimenting with simple Events whose outcomes are only directed at you and no other, as those situations involving others require more study. Keep track of your progress and decide if you are already to up your game. If you don't try out the Sorcery, you will not know if it works and you will not know your level of readiness.

Staying in the Agreement

A surgeon has to have an agreement with the goal to sustain life. Even if the patient going into surgery is thought to have a fifty-fifty chance, the surgeon is less likely to be successful if any power is given to the fifty percent that the patient will die, as that just increases the odds for death. A one hundred percent focus has to be applied to the fifty percent chance of life.

I have an associate who is a surgeon. I admire his work and discuss these materials with him whenever he is available to do so. I ask him about the experience of cutting into a living human being for the purpose of altering their anatomy for the outcome of increased life potential. He is a cardiac surgeon. He has been performing open-heart surgery since 1976, and he says the following:

"I remember the first surgery I conducted as the lead surgeon. The patient was a twenty-seven year old, a man with two young sons. As I cut into his chest with my scalpel, I noticed his blood seeping out of the incision and into the open air to die. I thought to myself, 'I better get this right because I just killed him a little bit more.' The surgery went fine and he went on to raise his sons. The thing is the blood though. Here I am thirty years later and every time I cut into a patient, I think exactly the same thing. Time and all the activity in the room take a moment and pause when the first blood appears. Everyone in the room stands up straight. It is the warning shot that something critical has begun to happen. I have seen that first blood thousands of times and it still surprises me, still makes me think I better get this right."

Blood, as it escapes our bodies, creates a moment of pause, a distinct human reaction that does not occur in the appearance of any other liquid or in any other context. Even thought there are variances in the manner of the reaction, human beings react in a powerful way when Blood appears. I truly perceive that **having a reaction to bleeding is the one and only Cultural Universal.**

Tools

I don't embrace tools. Tools are crutches. I do have an agreement that there are items—components perhaps—that accelerate the force of Sorcery and that champion your effort by enhancing the communication between you and the energy. That is not the same as a tool, because, in my language for the thing, a tool has made itself necessary, stating that the job cannot be done without it and requires a force from **outside of the self**. I offer instead the occasional use of components as a chosen catalyst.

Magnets, for example, are components. We are already part of the magnetic equation, so the addition of more magnets enhances **that which is already coming from**

within. This is why Sorcery works so efficiently and garners such fear, unlike the use of glittering of candles and the clasping of hands. Pretty and safe and fairy wings do not induce the connection to—or the control of—dangerous and forceful energies. Putting a knife in a cup (athame and chalice as Wiccans and others call them) is the use of tools because they bring something that functions **outside** of the realm which we already possess in the self, supporting the idea that our power comes from without rather than within.

IF YOUR POWER IS A COMBINATION OF TOOLS, OUTSIDE FORCES, DIVINITIES AND DOGMA, THEN YOU HAVE NO POWER, YOU ARE MERELY A COMPONENT IN AN EQUATION THAT *YOU BELONG TO*, RATHER THAN ONE THAT *BELONGS TO YOU*.

Belonging to anything is deadly to Sorcery. Sorcerers have no masters, and tools can become masters. Tools become bulky distractions and excuses for chaos, failure, and the giving away of our power to some object that is suddenly thought to be necessary in the transmission of desire into actualization. **All you need is pulsing inside of you.**

Now that I have written sufficiently about that which we do not need, what *do* we need? We need to ride the bike with no hands. We need only the forceful energy of our own power and our Blood, our Sacred Elixir, to be the method of delivery. The talismanic objects I offer and use are only **focus items,** things that remind us of the presence of Sorcery. It doesn't matter where you get these things, these objects; all that matters is how you use them. If talismans of some sort help you to remember to focus and stay in the work, or they work with you to streamline your energy, then they are fine for a while. If they are **necessary** to accomplish the work, throw them away immediately as they have tricked you into believing they hold a greater power than your Sacred Elixir. **Catalysts, not crutches.**

Sleeping Amongst the Dead

If you are saying that you are a Necromancer, Blood Sorceress, or Death-Worker, utilizing the Disincarnates in your work, and yet you have not slept amongst the dead, then one of three things has happened:

1. You have just not yet come to grips with that which is necessary—and that can be fixed through learning and accepting what is necessary. Or...
2. You are fooling yourself, and the underlying cause of that self-deception may or may not be fear-based. Or...
3. You might just be a poser. Posers are like backup singers; they rarely move to the front. Posers will carry this book around as an accessory, at best, to unnerve others, and will never grow to become Sorcerers. That is just fine with me.

Taking Inventory

Have you done everything you can possibly think of to perform your Sorcery Event in the fullest way to make it work? Have you slept amongst the dead? Have you harvested your Sacred Elixir and learned to control your fear? Have you listened to me and anyone else you feel is relevant in this field? I ask you this because by the time you come to me to troubleshoot, I want to know that you are not wasting my time with a clear hole in the inventory of what you should have and could have tried to the best of your personal ability.

And just for the record......

No, there is no way to be a Blood Sorcerer and not bleed.

When people come to me and want to study with me, I tell them this: If you are not willing to do the things that must be done to become a Blood Sorcerer or a Necromancer, then I will assist you by performing Sorcery Events for you, but I will not teach you. This work is not for the timid, or fearful, or squeamish. *If you aren't willing to put your own blood into your ink and sleep amongst the dead*—and I remind you that these are not options, they are *requirements*—then this is not your path and I am not your teacher.

Fearlessness

Fearlessness—what does it really mean to be fearless? I can enter a room full of demons alone and make the confrontation happen and win. I enter with an absolute agreement that it is me or the demon, that only one of us is coming out the victor and it isn't going to be the demon. There are no grey areas or near successes here. **Demons shoot live rounds**—if you will—and there is no way to partially win. I have been hit, shoved, burnt, had flour thrown in my face, listened to screaming so loud my ears hurt, and (my personal favorite) hit with flying books and other household objects. Fear would have gotten me killed.

The work will not wait for you if fear stops you from harvesting your Sacred Elixir or if you still have concerns about religion and karma. If today you want to do fertility Sorcery for yourself or others, but you are not willing to do it now—in real time—then you are not willing to do fertility Sorcery. Sounds simple but in a world where we give our children prizes and medals just for showing up, I tell you this isn't that sort of game and the only available prize is total success. No silver or bronze medals are offered. If you are not willing to be fearless and sit in the dark amongst the disincarnate when you cannot yet see them and they can see you, then you are not moving forward and this isn't for you.

This work is not to be done hidden away in the corner and it is not made to wait.

SORCERY HAS AN EXTREME EGO OF ITS OWN AND THAT IS HOW ITS MAGNIFICENCE BRINGS FORWARD SUCH EXTREME RESULTS.

If you say you want to be a priest or rabbi, someone in your life will rally around you and congratulate you, and make a fuss about your great passion and determination. But if you express that in your work you must traverse amongst the dead and become adept in the art of Blood Sorcery, then you will not be met with the same enthusiasm and may be considered delusional—or worse (although it is clear that the procedures of preparing for communion a Catholic mass does not stray far from the description of Blood Sorcery).

If your daily work or some aspect of your life requires that you stay in the grey area about Sorcery and you want to be a Sorcerer, then deal with it. Denial is denial and if you have to openly lie, you are living in denial. On the other hand, if you are simply living in a place of silence and privacy about your work, that is very different than living in a lie.

DEMONWORKS

This section offers Demon-related solutions for a few of the Sorcery Events in this book. A few months after the publication of this book I will release Volume Two, *Demonworks: The Stygian Manual*. That book will offer a complete treatment on the subject of Demons and how to handle them, use them in your work, combat them, and how to seek and make agreements with Attending Demons.

The following are the supplementary Demonworks materials mentioned throughout the "Sorcery Events" chapter.

SORCERY EVENT #1: To Heighten Sorcery Abilities

PROCEDURE #2 (of Sorcery Event #1)—Make a paintbrush from a few strands of your hair acquired from the left temple. (Tape or tie the strands to a toothpick or small piece of wood). Using any of the three bloods, draw stick figures of your ancestors on parchment. Using a sharp knife cut through the stick figures at their waistlines. Burn the lower half completely and smear the ashes from the lower half on the faces in the remaining upper half. Place the parchment under your bed and ask demons to reconnect you to your ancestors.

SORCERY EVENT #7: For Physical Strength

PROCEDURE—Add drops of this Sacred Elixir to red ink. Choose demon sigils that speak to you. Draw them and burn them. Take the ash and redraw them on the weakest part of your body. A demon will join you for a brief amount of time and tell you which physical attributes require strengthening and how you should proceed. The demon may also advise you about your overall ability to perform this work based on your current strength.

SORCERY EVENT #10: To Cause Physical Suffering and Slow Degeneration of an Enemy

PROCEDURE—Make a handprint on parchment from the Elixir using half of each hand so the print appears to have pinkies on both sides and no thumbs. Burn the edges of the parchment. Roll it into a scroll. Summon Demons by staying awake until you can no longer do so, keeping the scroll close to your body. Sleep alone in your bed in the quiet until you naturally arise. When you arise there will be an ink/grey dust in the scroll. You will see it if you look closely at the surface of the parchment. Scrape it off with a knife whose blade is sharp and preferably curved at the tip. Make a new harvest of the Elixir from the same place and mix it with the dust. Add it to black ink and write a note to the intended saying, "It was me and it will be me." Deliver it and burn the scroll. Add the remaining ash to the ink. Keep the ink for additional uses at another time.

SORCERY EVENT #14: To Access Attending Demons

PROCEDURE—This is the goal of so many Sorcerers and students of Sorcery. Accessing Attending Demons is a process done over 14 nights. The Sacred Elixir is drawn from *over the heart* and should only be done in the watchful care of a teacher. On occasion a Sorcerer will gain Attending Demons without this ritual. When that does not occur, this ritual is necessary. It is powerful Demonwork and should never be attempted alone. I am intentionally offering only this basic comment and not the entire ritual. If you feel you are ready for Attending Demons, contact me directly to discuss the potential performing of this ritual.

SORCERY EVENT #27: To Gain Health (Physical)

PROCEDURE—The absolute purest way to do this is to make an incision on the balls of both feet and smear the Sacred Elixir from one foot onto the other and vice versa. Perform this procedure three nights in a row, each time falling asleep as the Sacred Elixir dries. In each of the three mornings scrape off the Blood and add it into a mixture of red and black ink and a few drops of red wine. Invent or choose a sigil representing the demon that inhabits you and is keeping you unwell. (Yes, you can use this for diagnosed maladies; we are utilizing Demonworks here and demons are quite helpful when asked to latch onto dis-ease, as the energy of sickness feeds them—like leeches to blood and maggots to rotted flesh.) Using the ink mixture, draw the sigil on animal flesh. Sleep for one night with the drawn sigil. The next day, when the sun is directly over you (it doesn't matter if it is cloudy, this is a gravitational issue), place the sigil face up on a metal surface towards the sun. Leave it there until the sun sets. In the evening when the moon is directly above you, bury the sigil face down in a place where death has occurred on a tragic level (a house fire where an entire family was lost or something of that sort of magnitude). Bring yourself to tears as you bury it. You will become well.

HARVESTING THE ELIXIR

There is only one basic rule and it applies to both obtaining your own Elixir and when harvesting for/from another:

> **GET THE ELIXIR OUT OF THE BODY AND INTO SOME**
> **TYPE OF VESSEL**
> **IN THE LEAST INVASIVE WAY**

Here are some Harvesting recommendations: (The mechanics of *how* to collect it, and how to store it will be covered in the next section):

1. Drawn and Stored

Have your Sacred Elixir drawn or learn how to do it for yourself. Some phlebotomists will do this work and not ask you the purpose of the drawing. Ask them to bring tubes that do not have any chemicals such as preservatives or coagulants. Either way, keep vials of the Sacred Elixir in your freezer, labeled with the point on your body from which it was drawn. Yes, there is a greater value to freshly drawn Elixir but, as that is not always practical, better to have it ready than not. Sorcery is often a sudden response so it is better to have it available. Remember that the Sacred Elixir will expand when frozen so leave room in containers for expansion.

You may also refrigerate the Elixir. If you do, it will begin to significantly decompose within forty-eight hours or so, and it will move further and further away from living Elixir—by which I mean as decomposition begins, the Elixir becomes more suitable for work with Demons and the Disincarnate than the Science of Sorcery.

2. Immediate Sacred Elixir

It is always best, of course, to use Sacred Elixir that has just been released from its life within your vessels. To harvest immediate Elixir, I suggest the Sorcerer have a supply of lancets as this is an exercise in harvesting Sacred Elixir not a challenge of pain. **(Releasing the Elixir for pain is another area of this work and is touched upon in Section 4, Puncture.)** Lancets can be purchased online and are usually for sale for people who test their blood sugar. Most do not go very deep and do not provide a great deal of flow of the Sacred Elixir unless you are particularly thin-skinned.

Press the point of the lancet on the desired entry point hard and swiftly. To get a greater flow, push deeper, or use the sharp edges of the lancet to make a wider cut. Depending on how deep you go, and on which part of the body, you will get anywhere from a few drops to a short flow. DO NOT PUNCTURE BLOOD VESSELS with lancets unless you DESIRE, are PREPARED for, and can HANDLE the extraordinary flow of the Elixir. It is best not to do that sort of harvesting while alone as it is important to remember that what comes out is no longer available for your body to use and you may become weak, disoriented or pass out. If you have punctured a blood vessel and you become unconscious, you could die from exsanguination.

3. Harvest by Blade

When the manner in which the cut is made is part of the directive ("make a three inch incision," for example), use either a lancet, a sterilized box cutter, matt knife, very sharp sacrificial knife or blade, or, ideally, a scalpel. Be advised that an incision is NOT a slash. An incision begins with a point of pressure on the skin with the sterile blade, and a movement under pressure until the skin parts and the Elixir releases. It ends with a very deliberate stop and lifting away of the blade. Never use this method near large Blood vessels— neck, inner thigh, wrists, armpits, calves or anywhere you can see or feel large vessels. Great Sorcerers own a good anatomy book so that we know where NOT to cut. I suggest *Grey's Anatomy* or the *Circulatory System Coloring Book*. The illustrations are most helpful.

4. Puncture

Puncture is utilized for moments where **pain is desired** in order to get closer to the disincarnate who have a history of extraordinary pain either in the moment of death or due to previous lifestyle or illness. One use would be when you are attempting to see a homicide or violent action or situation through the eyes of an individual who died a horrific death. Pain is also required in the Sorcery Event of trading years of your life to save someone who is dying. There are dozens of additional Sorcery Events that require pain, some of which will be in the next book of this series.

Puncture is done with a round-end needle or a sacred punch. The instrument must be a thick, dull-edged type, like a tapestry needle that is round ended and meant to be used on canvas with preexisting holes; or use a hole punch meant for thin fabric. I have seen other dull points in usage as well such as vintage awls and other leather-working tools. When using vintage tools, make sure there is no rust on the tool as that could result in the need for a tetanus shot.

This is the method for puncture: Use a pen or a bit of eyeliner (makeup is hypoallergenic and less likely to cause a physical reaction) to make a dot to mark the desired target spot. Generally speaking it is good practice to keep in mind the intention of the use of the Elixir which will be harvested, but this is especially true with puncture. Hold the needle several inches above the dot, exhale fully and spear the dot. Just as mentioned in number three, do not use this method on or near Blood vessels. Be prepared with a collection method as Puncture delivers a larger amount of the Elixir and there will be a loss of Elixir if you are not prepared ahead of time.

5. Accidental or Spontaneous Instance of the Release of the Sacred Elixir

In Blood Sorcery a spontaneous instance is one where the Elixir has picked up a tainted yet invigorated energy from the events which caused the release. If you are injured or bleeding for some unplanned reason, collect the Sacred Elixir. It is very valuable and unique in this form as it is a spontaneous instance. The physics of the thing really show up in this case. The fear or stress or hostility in the blood from this type of release makes this Elixir extraordinarily valuable as a potent serum for revenge and justice Sorcery Events, as well as events that require the manipulation of time. Any Elixir collected from an accident is a result of a sudden, unplanned experience providing jolted Blood, which is very useful. The next section talks about how to collect the Elixir so I will not add that here.

6. Menstrual Sacred Elixir

Collect every bit you can... Share with a male Sorcerer you respect. Trade it for semen so everyone has what they need.

7. Harvested from Medical Procedures

If you are about to have any medical procedure, even dental, ask for all Sacred Elixir, tissue (priceless in this work), Sacred Elixir soaked gauze and other materials to be saved for you in an agreed-upon vessel or biohazard container with no preservatives or coagulants. This is offered to members of Orthodox religions who believe that every effort to bury the body in its entirety should be made. Why shouldn't you have the same rights? I will discuss preserving these materials in the next section.

COLLECTING AND PRESERVING THE ELIXIR AND BIOLOGICALS

The Sacred Elixir

The Sacred Elixir is most vibrant and powerful when the least time and distance has passed between harvest and use. The ultimate usage would be poured right from your body onto the body of the recipients of the Sorcery. Don't mistake this work for vampirism as the two are completely unrelated and actually opposite of one another. For us, Blood must leave the Sacred Vessel; for Vampyre, the blood must enter their Sacred Vessel. Think of the flow of the Sacred Elixir as you may see the power of attraction between magnets and think of time as distance. The closer the magnets the more powerful the pull. The more recently harvested the Elixir, the more potent the Sorcery.

Allow yourself to see the body as a large magnet and the Sacred Elixir as a smaller one buried within. They are attached, bound in force. As one is pulled from the other, you can still feel the pull between them until the crucial moment when just enough distance stands between them and there is no longer a pull of any kind. Time and decomposition is like the space between these magnets. Yet a certain caution still exists as we know if they were ever to find themselves alongside each other again, closer to one another in any way, they would once again join forces and become a more powerful magnet together. Blood has the same property, the same reconnection. It is, however, not visible with the naked eye but only by the result of the Sorcery for which this re-connective property is utilized.

THAT gives us the parameters for how to collect the Sacred Elixir and THAT is the Blood Sorcery.

When I hold the Sacred Elixir in my hand I find myself in the presence of greatness and I am honored to have this fluid with which to perform Sorcery. So three questions arise in my mind when I am collecting the Sacred Elixir:

What is Death?—as it pertains to the Elixir in my hand.

When is Death?—is there a point at which the Elixir is no longer viable enough for this work?

Is Death reversible?—does giving this weakening Elixir to the task of Sorcery provide it with new life?

If I were to attempt to answer those questions I may say:

What is Death?—the non-availability of choice, so there must be variables that make the harvested Elixir unstable and in need of guidance from the One who will use it in ritual.

When is Death?—when choices can no longer be made, the Sorcery one performs lingers and the outcome may be based on not only the Elixir itself but its relationship with the practitioner

Is Death reversible?—I have yet to prove death happens so the experiments continue……

In the Moment of Ritual

Ritual begins at the moment of harvest. *Do not* make the mistake of thinking that harvest is only preparation. **Harvest is the ritual**. The action of and moment of the harvesting of the Sacred Elixir creates the ACTION of bleeding or being drawn, and is powerful in and of itself. Does the Sacred Elixir know what is happening? Does the DNA tell it a story of death and dying? In that fragment of time (providing one can imagine such a fraction), in the moment it leaves the body—the housing—Blood is in the strongest phase of the power. The energy caused when the Sacred Elixir is struggling on the border of life and Death (choice or no choice) is enormous. It struggles like a captive animal and in that struggle it releases powerful energy. It's all physics.

That being said...

Some Sorcery, like the raising of the dead, or creating a cast (which J.K. Rowling calls a Horcrux) and making a trade-off of living time for something vital, MUST be done by that sort of Sacred Elixir: just released and waiting for its cue to remain alive or die. It gives up its right to choose when this action occurs. When harvesting the Sacred Elixir, read carefully through the ritual as it may require that the Elixir be spilled directly from the wound onto the ritual item while the memory of your heartbeat still exists within cell memory.

BE COMPLETELY PREPARED AHEAD OF TIME OR YOU WILL LOSE THE MOST VITAL PART OF THE RITUAL— THE HARVESTING.

For example, later in this book you will find a ritual that requires you to make a slit in a specific body part and "collect" the Sacred Elixir by rolling a candle into the incision, covering it with the collected Blood, and carving right through the Sacred Elixir onto the candle. For this you must have all components ready at once. Another will ask you to drip the Sacred Elixir directly onto a grave or onto cremains, or an effigy doll or into a potion, etc... **Know the ritual fully before you begin.**

Now onto preserving the Elixir and other biologicals—

Preserving the Elixir as Liquid

This method is useful for all types of harvests, including Sacred Menstrual Elixir and accidental or unexpected release of the Sacred Elixir.

Keep a supply of small vials that can be frozen. Always use glass and remember to only fill the vial or small jar (oil bottles, dram, half dram, etc., are good) only half way if you are freezing the liquid. Label the vial with the date and location on your body from which the Sacred Elixir was released. If you want to use it soon, refrigerate it but remember, just like meat, it will deteriorate in less than forty-eight hours. Frozen Sacred Elixir lasts much longer before putrefaction sets in. My years as an autopsy technician and an embalmer, and now as a mummifier have left me with an understanding of the speed of decomposing human tissue.

In the case of accidental Blood, I carry vials with me everywhere as one never knows what type of opportunity one will encounter. It is also valuable to carry a cooling pack, like the ones that can be activated by shaking or breaking, (they are available in pharmacies and meant for injuries that require a cold compress) and a plastic bag or padded envelope. This may sound extreme now but should the instance occur, you will wish you had a collection kit.

Pipettes

Keep a supply of these tiny glass tubes. They are useful to store small amounts of the Sacred Elixir and can be kept refrigerated. Poke them into a piece of Styrofoam and label the foam as the pipettes themselves are too tiny to label. Use only glass ones. Some are able to be sealed at both ends by holding the tips over a candle flame and either melting the glass tube flat, pinching it or bending it over with something that can stand the heat such as tweezers. This creates a sealed tube you can carry as a talisman or as a hidden port-able supply.

Storing the Elixir in Gauzes

This, too, is a very useful method for collecting Sacred Menstrual Elixir or accidental Sacred Elixir. Collect Sacred Menstrual Elixir on pads or tampons, and accidental or unexpected Sacred Elixir on bandages, tissue or fabric.

Drying the Collected Elixir for Use

Place gauze pieces containing the Sacred Elixir in a plate covered with salt. Table salt or kosher salt will do. Rest the items on top of the salt and let them stand in open air in a well-ventilated place. Keep them away from pets, as they are perceived by animals as meat, and your pets will eat them. After a week or so, check to see if the Sacred Elixir is dry and hard. Place fresh chunk salt in a brown paper bag, making sure to cover the bottom surface area. Cover the mixture with a thin layer of tissue paper so that the dried bits do not get the salt on them. Cut away all gauze that does not contain any Sacred Elixir. Cut the portion containing the Sacred Elixir into small pieces. Place them in the bag and leave the top opened. They are, of course, usable at any point in this process but are completely dried after a few months. Semen and other biologicals (such as any other body fluid, including tears), can also be stored this way.

Uses for Dried Sacred Elixir and the Issues of Quantity

These dried pieces are usable in incense as well as talismanic materials.

To use in incense, grind them in a mortar and pestle and add them to the formula you have created. Use them spar-ingly as their content is heavy, by which I mean that human blood is just as powerful in a small amount as it is in a large amount. When one pricks a finger the gut reaction is the same to the Sacred Elixir itself as it is to a larger gash. The situation may be more serious from one to another, but the reflex response is the same. Blood Sorcery is proved by that reflex response. As physics and Sorcery are so intimately entwined, it is just that principle that drives the use of quantity. In the case of incense, less is exactly the same as more.

Talismans are formed by adding a catalyst of dried Sacred Elixir to an object (such as lockets and fabric sachets or whatever works in a given situation) in which to carry or present them. Any talisman is further served by the use of the Sacred Elixir as part of its content. I have placed pieces of dried Sacred Elixir into dolls, pins, poison rings, sewn small talismans into a myriad of other types of Sorcery Elements, and, by request, even placed and sewn them deeply into dreadlocks. The individual used his hair as a powerful talisman, keeping an Elixir marker for each of his Sorcery Events as if it were a living journal of his work. We Sorcerers are very passionate about our work...

IT IS BEST THAT THE SACRED ELIXIR

BE SET DEEP WITHIN THE TALISMAN

SO THAT IT IS NOT TOUCHED.

+++++++++++++++++++++++++

THINK OF YOUR OWN SACRED ELIXIR AS

RELIC QUALITY,

AND YOU WILL BEGIN TO UNDERSTAND

USES FOR IT THAT DID NOT

COME TO YOU PREVIOUSLY.

POST MEDICAL/SURGICAL PROCEDURES AND AUTOPSIES

I can tell you this as absolute fact, as I have seen it done many times in my service at the Office of the Chief Medical Examiner: members of Orthodox faiths are permitted to have a representative witness an autopsy of a member of their faith and obtain any biological materials from the autopsy procedure that the Medical Examiner's office would discard (or wash away), if it is their belief that the biological materials must remain with the body for burial.

As Sorcerers you have the same right to those opinions and to the appropriate handling of those biologicals as they pertain to your human form and the human form of other Sorcerers and family members.

When someone in your life has died in a curious or unexpected manner and an autopsy is scheduled, if you feel, much like I do, (and like Aleister Crowley did—just a point of interest, the rest of his theosophy aside), that being separated from your biologicals at this point in death is inappropriate, then demand this right to retain those materials either on your behalf or on the behalf of another Sorcerer.

How to Collect the Materials

Materials obtained from autopsies and medical procedures should be collected in containers agreed upon in advance, as it is vital that the biologicals NOT be placed in containers with preservatives or anti-coagulants if you are intending to use them for the purpose of Sorcery. Biomedical containers are available and can also be provided by the medical team doing the procedure or by the Medical Examiner or coroner.

You may be looked upon in a disparaging way but that is irrelevant to the task at hand. It is helpful as Sorcerers if we have letters in place expressing these desires should a situation arise unexpectedly. As Sorcerers be as ready as you can.

HARVESTING THE BIOLOGICALS OF OTHERS

Much like *The Anarchist Cookbook*, I am simply presenting the materials; I am not offering a treatment on how to set your moral compass. I am a Blood Sorceress and one of the things one can do when utilizing the art of Blood Sorcery is to use the Elixir of others.

Let us be honest with ourselves and acknowledge that there are only two categories under which these materials can be collected: Consensual and Non-Consensual. Third party collection without the permission of the host is still non-consensual. If someone brings you Semen from her lover and he is not aware of the collection of that Semen, it is still non-consensual. Again, I state this not as a moral judgment but for clarity. Admit your choices at least to yourself.

Consensual Collection

All of the same rules apply when collecting the Elixir from another, either to use their biologicals for your work or to do work on their behalf. When doing work for another, the use of their own biologicals or Sacred Elixir greatly increases the probability that the desired outcome and potential of the Sorcery Event will be an exact hit. Another type of consensual collection is trading biologicals: for example, Sacred Menstrual Elixir, breast milk or Placenta for Semen. Semen is best preserved through Flaking.

Flaking

I saved this preservation technique for now instead of including it in the earlier section on preservation because it seems most important as a separate section. To appropriately Flake Semen or the Sacred Elixir, these materials should be smoothed onto a glass, allowed to air dry and are then flaked off. This is best done with another smooth nonporous item such as another piece of glass for the smoothing and a long thin blade for Flaking. While Flaking off the materials from the glass, make a tent of tin foil or paper so that bits of the Flaked materials don't escape the process. Flake directly into a clean bag.

The flakes should be stored in a dry glass container. They are likely to keep a significant portion of their effectiveness as they have not encountered contamination and have been stored promptly. I will revisit Flaking in the chapter, "Scrying".

Non-Consensual Collection of
Another Individual's Biologicals

Hair and nails are simple to collect as all one has to do is be in proximity to obtain hair and observe the habits of the individual to obtain nails. Location and use of hair (head, chest, pubic area etc.) apply to Sorcery Events just as does the harvested Sacred Elixir. Use the Sorcery Event section as a guide to obtain the hair closest to the area that will provide the best outcome for the Sorcery Event at hand. Hair is, of course, more effective with roots.

On the subject of skin cells: they are dead upon release and therefore not as useful as other biologicals. The value of hair and nails is the same as they are both a product of dead cells and are even less valuable than skin cells because they have been dead the longest. (The one exception: hair and nails are better for divination as they tell a story about the events in which the subject has participated over time.) They were not alive at the time of the harvesting so they are at least one degree away from the power of the Sacred Elixir. That said, it is better to have them than to have no biologicals at all.

When using nails, it is best to know from which finger the nail was harvested. That may be important information as it pertains to certain Sorcery Events. The thumb is the most masculine and the masculinity moves toward femininity the closer to the pinky, with the pinky being the most feminine. The right hand is for pushing away and the left for drawing in. That is really all you need to know. Your instincts can fill in the rest.

Menstrual Blood and Semen are the strongest fluids available. Trade them with a Sorcerer of the opposite gender to provide all opportunities for yourselves.

IF YOU CAN OBTAIN MENSTRUAL BLOOD OR SEMEN FROM THE PERSON YOU ARE WORKING ON, THE HIT WILL BE EXACT.

SEXUAL FLUIDS

Depending on the kind of sex you are having, biologicals produced during sex can be obtained in a number of ways and you may have to be creative. If necessary, wipe them off yourself onto something non-porous or suck them out and spit into something made of glass. Not simple, but necessary if you want these materials. Breast milk can also be obtained this way.

Materials that are wiped off of yourself allow for less contamination if they are not **scraped** off your body, just gently collected, so that they contain few, if any, of your skin cells. Flake these materials for best preservation.

Semen that is not available to be collected topically is best collected via oral sex. Semen that has been inside any other orifice has a greater chance of having too much of your more potent biologicals in it through mingling. If it is obtained from another orifice use it only if necessary. Semen from inside of a condom is usable ONLY if the condom does not contain spermicide. Spermicides destroy the viable powerful content of Semen. Ejaculation onto your body and collected by rolling a glass or scooping up with a water glass is purest. If you truly want these materials YOU figure out how to explain that in the moment.

Flake the Semen. Semen is always best preserved by this method.

Non-Consensual Sacred Elixir Collection

It is tricky to get another individual's Sacred Elixir without consent. Play a sex game, offer to shave the person, bite and spit in some kind of role play—whatever is needed. DO NOT drug them or get them drunk as enough drugs or alcohol to knock them out will contaminate the Elixir and render it either useless, or worse, able to confuse or change its purpose in your Sorcery Event. If the intended is getting a piercing or a tattoo, offer to help clean up. The treasure is on the gauze. In this situation you may have to deal with antiseptics diminishing the product. Again, diminished Sacred Elixir is better than no Sacred Elixir at all.

The rest of this matter is up to you. If you want these materials badly enough you will get them...

SCRYING

Scrying in Necromancy

Divination is often considered as a principle reason for raising the Dead. A Sorcerer can communicate with the disincarnate by seeing their image in a scrying device and, in a way, capture the disincarnate in time. Sacred Elixir Sorcery puts a particularly unique point of view on the subject of baiting as it applies to scrying. The Elixir itself is used as bait and the properties of the disincarnate dictate the type and quantity of Sacred Elixir needed to facilitate this communication. You will be using your own Sacred Elixir for this process so if you are consorting with the disincarnate for a particular Sorcery Event, harvest your Elixir for the particular Sorcery Event you intend. (See the chapter "Thirty Sorcery Events and How to Read Them".)

Raising and Communicating with the Disincarnate can be done in many ways. Scrying allows the Sorcerer to make the connection through all sorts of devices, including those existing in nature as well as everyday objects.

My philosophy is that having too many devices or tools can be a crutch. Water, wind, the elements themselves, can provide opportunities for spontaneous tools to assist in your practice, avoiding the accumulation of tools (and therefore avoiding clutter). Remember: when using tools or devices, allow yourself to see them in everything so that you will not be bound by convention or by a catalogue from the local witchery. To stretch the point, even the nervous energy of others can be a tool, a source of additional power. This would be considered a reflective device as it involves the utilization of the reflection of energy. Think of yourself as a nomad or as someone of great skills whose tools are all that is around them, available in real time.

> **REALISTICALLY SPEAKING, YOUR *'TOOLKIT'* NEED ONLY CONSIST OF THE EDUCATION THAT YOU HAVE PROVIDED YOURSELF ON THESE MATERIALS, YOUR MIND, YOUR SACRED ELIXIR AND THE OCCASIONAL SHARP BLADE AND SMOOTH SURFACE.**

There is nothing more ridiculous to me than a New Age catalogue of magical devices: knives (referred to as athames), skull-shaped goblets and specialty glasses for scrying. To scry, one needs a smooth surface and if you look around right where you are at this very moment, you will most likely see a dozen choices. Scrying, like all Sorcery, existed well before specialized witchy supply companies and it will exist long after. As previously mentioned, life is filled with basic scrying devices; therefore, seeking out basic scrying devices wherever you are at any given moment is a perfect example of this way of working and allows a free-dom of movement amongst Sorcerers.

I love glass. After the Sacred Elixir and magnets, glass is the most useful device as it is everywhere, and is reflective, non-absorbent and powerful. Its magnificence is a result of its manifestation, as it exists only because of a heat-related transformation. It is all physics, plus time and willingness.

To scry, use a mirror, or a flat piece of glass, or a window. A glass TV screen can be useful as well if there is no other choice, and the darkness may even help you see clearly without distraction. Prepare ahead of time some black ink by adding several drops of your Elixir and spread the mix across the glass. Though not absolutely necessary the black ink adds a depth that the human eye responds well to. This work can be done entirely in Sacred Elixir if you have the quantity available. Remember that quality is not a requirement for events such as scrying so save your Elixir by using only a few drops and utilize black or red ink.

While the surface is still wet, write the following words in it with your finger. Do not be concerned if the words are not readable as it is the act of writing that is relevant.

MODICAT VOGOR DEVET-T CIM

Say these 'words' with as much vibration as you can while touching the glass. Repeat several times. These are simply a group of vibratory tones, not some ancient Latin phrase, so save your research time. Speaking these 'words' in a low, vibrating voice activates the glass. I found these words by listening to the feedback from my own scrying events (that is, the scrying surface itself told me the vibratory tones). How did I scry without them the first time? I hummed and did what I do to attract the disincarnate. While scrying, this was what I heard from the glass over time when I left the portal opened at all times and the disincarnate tried to get my attention:

MIC T-TEVED ROGOV TACIDOM

It occurred to me that if this was what the glass needed to open up the communication, then the reverse of it would allow me to vibrate in from my side of the portal. I experimented with this process many times over and found that my assumptions were correct. This passage back and forth can be traversed by a vibration connection through sound and the Sacred Elixir.

> **THE VIBRATION YOUR VOICE CAUSES THROUGH THE GLASS, PLUS THE IRON IN YOUR SACRED ELIXIR—WHICH ACTS AS A MAGNETIC CONNECTION TO THE DISINCARNATE—CREATES AN EQUATION THAT IS SOLID AND EXTRAORDINARILY USEFUL.**

Once you feel the glass has picked up the vibration, concentrate on the center of the glass and 'listen' with all of your senses. Stop being in your own way—don't try or imagine, just listen and be inside the glass. You will hear voices and see light and changing images in the glass. Do not get sidetracked or startled.

In this moment, go ahead and ask the questions you need to ask. Once you are satisfied with the conversation, close the portal by acknowledging the Disincarnate. Put your finger in your mouth, wet it and drag it through the ink/Sacred Elixir breaking the main section. That action ends the session. Then you can wash away the rest of the ink/Sacred Elixir or, if this has been a particularly memorable scrying session, **make a talisman** that will act as a catalyst for your next scrying session. Do the following to create that talisman:

Flake the mix off the glass and wear it in a vial as a talisman. Flaked crystals from the scrying session continue to vibrate if kept in glass. This may provide an opportunity for an ongoing portal opened to a particular disincarnate who chose to communicate with you during the scrying session. If that happens, you may also write the name of that disincarnate in the mixture when opening the portal.

Specific Scrying Glasses

To see the Disincarnate in a particular location, you can use Scrying Glasses just for this purpose. One type of powerful scrying glasses are the actual glasses that belonged to a child or young person who died a long and painful death through illness. Consider estate sales or develop friendships with nurses who deal with dying youth. If you do obtain a pair of these glasses, keep them in a safe and reverent place. (If you find that upsetting or macabre, then you are not meant for this work.) Surrounding yourself with the belongings of the Disincarnate has a magnetic effect, drawing more Disincarnate with that energy. The use of a dead child's belongings is just one example of how one may use items collected from the disincarnate in this work.

Put the glasses on and acknowledge the suffering of the deceased. Rarely is pain an asset, but this is one of the situations where it is. Take the glasses off, acknowledge the parents and caregivers of the child, and then harvest the Sacred Elixir from your right palm (if you are extremely courageous, use the Puncture method).

Coat the inside and outside of the lenses with smears of the Elixir applied in opposite directions. Let the Sacred Elixir dry thoroughly. Put the glasses on with your eyes closed and consciously allow the previous owner of the glasses, the deceased child, into your presence and ask for its assistance in the divination or other work at hand. Ask slowly and patiently as you are dealing with a child who died before developing into someone who can process questions quickly. The beauty of working with a dead child is that such a child is likely to ASK questions and is operating with an extremely pure curiosity. Therefore the information and communication flows freely back and forth, to the extent that you are able to stay open, fearless and welcoming.

A Disincarnate child may want to tell you a story. If you really want to be a Necromancer you will graciously accept this honor and show gratitude for the opportunity. Encourage the child into playing a game if you feel it will help to get your questions answered. All Disincarnate "single digit" (age nine and below) children are WATCHERS, which means that have stood by and absorbed all kinds of information from both the living and the Dead. A Disincarnate single digit may even be able to touch you as they have no belief that they cannot and tend to crave contact. If you show fear, the disincarnate child will interpret your fear as if they have misbehaved and they will never aid you again.

Lie or sit still in low comfortable light, as it is my experience that many disincarnate children are light sensitive. It is the most effective way to have the communication with the child. Films portraying disincarnate children dancing and playing in the sunlight are truly taking poetic license. The only ones I have encountered who are visible in that way are usually frustrated, disoriented, looking for someone or something, and not always clear that they are dead. Disincarnate children cannot handle burdens of any kind. They are NOT healers. Do not bother them with that work. They are shy and the purpose of your interaction with them is to build trust and have them spy on both the living and the Dead. They may be willing to develop a long-term relationship with you if you are a fearless Necromancer.

Scrying in Water:
The Still Water Scrying Pool

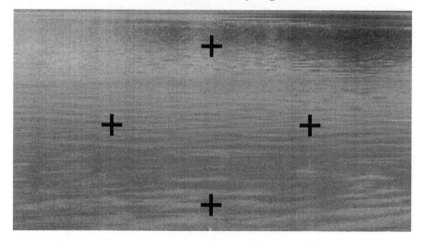

To open the Still Water Scrying Pool you must mix drops of Elixir from your left palm with a pure oil, and shake them together until they look as mixed as possible. As in the illustration, place one drop of Sacred Elixir into the water to form a diamond (make it a size that feels comfortable to you) and smear some in a downward motion from just below your chin to your heart. These actions will open the portal and you will see any number of faces of the Disincarnate moving through this water mirror. Close this portal by wiping through the "diamond" with one hand and, using your wet hand, wash away the smear you previously placed down your throat. As a gift to the disincarnate, pour any remaining Elixir/Oil mix into the water and walk away.

Scrying for the Truth

You can scry for the Truth through a lover's body fluids and/or Elixir. Collect the Sacred Elixir or biological and smear the fluid on the outside of a clear glass (best if it is one they drank from) or a glass bowl. When the fluid dries, fill the glass with water. Using the vibrational sounds MODICAT VOGOR DEVET-T CIM, ask to see the truth about a situation in which you believe you have been lied to; or ask for clarity where there may be confusion between yourself and another. The truth will present itself in the water. Flake off the biologicals and wear them in a glass vial. The person who told you the lie—or who is being ambiguous—will not be able to continue to lie to you. You may choose to follow up with a justice Sorcery Event.

PORTALS

Opening Portals

The number one question my students ask is: "How do I open the Portal?"

For those who do not yet live with—or do not desire to live with—a constantly (Eternally) open portal (one that allows the Disincarnate to be present at all times without boundaries), as I do, momentary portals can work for you. Most Necromancers choose to open Momentary Portals as needed and close them when the work is done. Very few of us live with Eternal Portals. Read this section carefully if you do not want to live amongst the disincarnate at all times, as they are not burdened with boundary issues. The next section will delve more deeply into the difference between the Momentary and Eternal Portals.

There are a few basic methods, but I must say that to be a Necromancer you must do that which anyone who wants to be anything does: You must be amongst the experts—in this case, the Disincarnate—and if possible, befriend another who can communicate with them. A mentor in this area is a powerful thing. I have had students who were not able to open a portal until I placed them within one and then they were able to do it on their own. Much of Blood Sorcery is taught that way.

Two Types of Portals:
Momentary and Eternal
Antimatter

Portals are everywhere. To open one all that is necessary is to find it and force upon it a moment of your energy which causes a full stop, a break in the movement of it. It is a combination of matter and antimatter and if we do not yet understand exactly what that is, then perhaps it is best that we accept it to be true for the purpose of this work. Einstein stated:

> "For every one billion particles of antimatter there were one billion and one particles of matter. And when the mutual annihilation was complete, one billionth remained—and that is our universe."

Physicists have struggled with why our universe is made up mostly of matter and not antimatter. Allow yourself some different thought here. What if you agreed to agree that we have no idea what the disincarnate that we see are made of. They do not have substance as they can pass through solids and no matter can do that in an absolute way without some physical conflict. So then, what are we left with that we can understand? Absolutely nothing. What if we allowed ourselves to not know but to participate anyway? That is the process of finding and opening portals.

I live with an Eternal Portal. The Disincarnate walk about in my life just as the living do, with the exception that they can enter my house, my bedroom, and anywhere they like whenever they like. I set rules and most of them follow. My Nine Attending Demons help keep it all in order, but in reality there is no downtime for me. Most will respect the rules and stay out of my bed when I sleep for a few hours. Most will respect my wishes if I tell them I cannot talk to them at a particular moment as I am well known amongst them and they all know I will do my best to give them their turn, especially if they have something interesting to offer. They have come to understand that it is better to treat me with reverence than to bully me. Some are vulgar and demanding and without boundaries. I ignore them and eventually they get frustrated and leave.

Occasionally one disincarnate will act as a leader, trying to create order, acting as a screener on my behalf, by sorting through the disincarnate and bringing those with the greatest needs to my attention. The one who does that always gets extra time with me as these are individuals who step up and take that responsibility. They know that taking this responsibility is the best way to get served by me as a matter of gratitude. Those are NOT my attending demons. They are intelligent opportunists and we all benefit from their strategy.

So from all of that experience, what I have come to understand is that the disincarnate are the same as they were when they lived in flesh and walked as we do now. Death has an effect on them, as they perhaps become more of who they were, by which I mean the frustration some of them experience and the freedoms others embrace bring out their personalities. They are more able to be themselves as if they are cured of inhibitions without the effects of alcohol. The longer I speak to them the more they will reveal themselves and their way of embracing death. I have learned a great deal from these interactions.

After reading all of that I suggest you ask: Do I want that for myself? Do I want to live amongst the needy walking-Dead every moment of my life? If you do (and maybe you can and maybe you can't) you must, in your life, live amongst Death as I have suggested throughout this book. Death is a big industry. Work in a place where death is received, volunteer in places where people have come to die, sleep in cemeteries—whatever you have to do as I have done for most of my life. If you are just beginning, collect graveyard dirt, pieces of headstones, touch a flower to the deceased at funerals (find busy wakes and just create a simple persona and visit; people rarely inquire as to how you knew the deceased) and press the flowers to their bodies to use later in rituals.

Steal from the beds of those who have just died. I suggest volunteering in a hospice or other medical services environments. Yes, just steal. Take a personal belonging or a bit of medical materials. Buy human bones and snip bits of hair from the dead whenever possible. One strand is the same as one hundred strands. Collect whatever you can that was there with the deceased in the moment of death, or anything that lingered with the body, or represents internment.

Cremains (created remains) are also useful but not as useful as items that were there when Death visited. As you collect these things you will find that some of them act as portal keys, baiting the disincarnate to walk through. Portals, like all things related to Necromancy, are an equation of skill + bait + willingness + applied physics such as magnetics.

CAUTION: If you open enough Momentary Portals, eventually you will find that the relationships you have developed with the Disincarnate **will produce an Eternal Portal and Attending Demons.** That is just how it goes. Repeatedly opening Momentary Portals is a slippery slope if you don't want an Eternal Portal, and a good strategy to strengthen your skills and awareness if you do.

Attending Demons—and Demons in general—will be the subject of my next book, Volume 2 in this series, *Demonworks, The Stygian Manual.* That being said I will say a bit about demons here, more as a cautionary tale.

IF YOU ARE NEW TO THE ART OF NECROMANCY, DEMONS ARE THE RIVAL GANG.

A Demon is not simply an angry or disturbed disincarnate. A demon is an amalgam, a group creation derived from the collection of tortured energies of multiple people and occasionally animals and situations.

> **DEMONS FORM WHEN THE DISAGREEABLE ENERGIES FIND ONE ANOTHER AND DEVELOP A RELATIONSHIP, THEN GATHER TOGETHER AND UTILIZE COMBINED ENERGY.**

The energy allows the tortured elements to bond and choose a leader amongst them. The leader can be one of the members from whom these destructive elements emerged, or it can be a new force fighting from within, wrestling amongst the ruffians in the group to emerge as a leader. Those are the most powerful because their internal conflict fuels them, keeping the heat within and churning it to develop stronger more intense energies. Their powerful forces create EMP (Electro-Magnetic Pulses). These pulses attach to sound waves and push outward, getting trapped in metal objects, allowing them to push into the air and move objects, even moving the air itself. Those are the skills of the demons who have made aggressive, physical contact with me. Those are the dangerous ones who can hold onto a physical place, inhabiting it with their hostility and causing grief for anyone who wishes to live there.

Their hostility is viral. They spin and leave a thin coating of black dust. If any of my readers have ever lived in a house that seemed ripe with hostility of an unknown origin, you may think back and remember that you took notice of how dusty and grimy things seemed, how no amount of cleaning could make the environment fresh. The air was never quite clear and the lights were never quite bright. Joy and playfulness seemed clouded like an outdoor event that encountered a rainy day. If you have had those experiences, you have lived amongst them, amongst Demons.

If you are new to this work, do not try to fight the demons yet. You may not survive the interactions. Do not do the work of cleaning Demons out of a structure of any kind as they are able to pull walls and objects down around you. This is not work for the novice, which brings me to the next subject.

Momentary Portals: Some of the Methods

1. Scrying

See the chapter on "Scrying".

2. Disincarnate Specific Portal

If you are in need of communication with a **specific person** who you knew personally, the way to access that person is to create an environment which will entice them into a moment you shared. Pick a SPECIFIC moment in memory (not a day or a week, but rather a single moment: the shortest most powerful memory you can remember sharing) and re-create it. It is important to pick a moment that you genuinely believe the Disincarnate in question will remember that way as well, or the entire approach is no more than you re-exploring a moment that means something to you. By specific moment I mean a moment that could have been caught in a snapshot: a particularly memorable kiss, a moment when a child laughed, a hug, a violent moment (anything passionate works well), a shared sexual moment (anything passionate works well), saying the same word at the same time and laughing…these are the moments that will bait the disincarnate as these are the moments they, too, mourn and crave.

Recreate the Scene

Set the stage to recreate the moment, bringing everything you can remember into place. Utilize the senses. I will list them in the order in which they have worked best for me at baiting the Disincarnate.

Scent is the most powerful, so recreate the scent as you remember it to have been in that exact moment. Remember you are reaching out to someone who needs to be baited, lured back. Perfumes, the smell of food cooking, even unpleasant scents, as long as they represent the moment you are recreating.

Next think about sound. This is the second most important route to bait the disincarnate. What did the moment sound like to you? What do you remember? Don't edit this moment. Include everything: the sound of the dishwasher, a smoke alarm that may have been beeping occasionally to remind you to change the battery, a song, a dripping faucet... Add whatever you can remember.

At this point, you will have the attention of the Disincarnate so address the sense of touch next but make it visible so it can still be a lure. What did the moment feel like? Wear what you were wearing—or not wearing if this was an intimate moment. Stroke the pillows on the chair the disincarnate sat in, fold a favorite towel, handle a particular utensil, use (or act as if you are using) a cell phone that belonged to this person. Explore other items that the individual held or felt close to such as a stuffed animal or a pet. Pets are most helpful because their lack of boundaries allow them to see the Disincarnate before you will. Set up touch from the point of view of the Disincarnate, not from the point of view of how it felt for you to touch them, unless you believe that receiving that touch would be the physical contact that is most likely to draw them to you.

Lastly, add the visual component, as you will probably at this point have them in the room. Visual components place last as you will have to already have lured the individual in, in order to create an opportunity for the Disincarnate to see what you have recreated.

I have left out taste because there has been no evidence in my vast experience that has proven to me that the ability to taste is retained by the disincarnate. I have even experienced resentment about this from a number of Disincarnate individuals so to avoid their hostility, I leave it out. The smell of their favorite food cooking is a lure, just leave it at that.

Now you must prepare the most powerful bait: the Sacred Elixir. It draws them as they miss the warmth in their bodies. They also miss the sense of danger. What is danger? It is ultimately the fear of death, of having death somewhere **in front** of us in our lives. It is that innate concern which keeps humans on edge and feeling to make sure we still have a pulse. Think about it: if that threat were removed, you could jump out of airplanes and confront the bad guys. It sounds like an amazing opportunity, but what is left once that thrill is played out? This is one of the reasons the disincarnate become so frustrated and join together as demons.

Prepare by using a lancet or other small blade. Open five spots on your body where your Sacred Elixir can escape. I use five because four never worked and five worked just as well as six or more, it is that simple. For locations, I suggest somewhere under your hair, the left upper inner arm, somewhere between the navel and genitals, the back of either thigh, and the top of either foot. DO NOT USE the bottom of the feet for this purpose or you will be inviting disincarnate with whom you are not familiar and also opening the portal for the possibility of attracting demons.

Lie down amongst the sights, sounds and scents of the moment and re-live it, asking the Disincarnate whose presence you desire to re-live it with you. Your Sacred Elixir— your Blood—is the most powerful bait. Once you hear and/or see the person you sought, tell them you will re-live the moment with them if they first answer your questions or do that which you have called them to do. That re-living is their payoff. You MUST have the courage to let them go as they will become trapped in this moment if it is pleasurable for them to be in it. Acknowledge them for coming to you. When the session is over, disarrange the scene and shower off the Elixir without scrubbing. Just running water—no soap.

3. Non-Specific Disincarnate:
Seeking the Assistance of Any Disincarnate
Who Will Provide the Information You Seek

In this situation you will be raising someone who will be asked for information, not personal interaction. This can be someone you never met or heard of, or someone you know **of** but do not personally know. For better success with this, I suggest you practice the Disincarnate Specific Portal (above) multiple times before trying this method, as successes in that type will grow your ability to move onto contacting and utilizing Disincarnate strangers.

Using a lancet, open an incision on your left thigh, just above the top of your knee. Collect most of the elixir wet (in a vessel) and collect the remainder by rolling a candle over the incision. (The color of the candle means nothing. I use black or purple for the comfort and focus I derive from those colors so that is my choice. This is Sorcery, not goddess worship, so throw away your candle color and moon phase charts. Roll the candle in the remaining Elixir from the incision and carve the words directly THROUGH the Elixir into the candle while saying them aloud, in a low vibratory tone:

GEDETT ESTAR PERSONA

Again these are only vibratory tones and are not Latin words or harborages of hidden meanings. The purpose of the candle is to add heat and illumination to the Sacred Elixir. It is all physics.

Pour a bit of the Elixir on a glass surface. Stand the candle up in the smear of Elixir, sit in front of this instant altar and repeat the words that are carved into the candle. DEMAND the Disincarnate to speak to you. Tap the bottom of the candle in smeared Elixir. Tapping is a noise that can be helpful to bait the Disincarnate in this situation. When the session is over, pick up the candle and snuff it by smashing the flame down into the smeared Elixir. Stay still until the scent of the extinguished flame burning your Sacred Elixir is gone.

CAUTION: IF YOU MOVE BEFORE THAT, YOU WILL BE IN THE FIRST STEP OF INVOKING RANDOM DEMONS WHICH I WILL NOT BE DISCUSSING IN THIS BOOK SO THERE WILL BE NO LIFE SAVING INFORMATION OFFERED HERE.

You are alone in the work. Sorcery is a solitary art—no matter how many sorcerers are in the room—because the power is personally driven. If you want to have what you desire, perform the rituals from this book.

4. Use of Location—A Component Creator

Go to a cemetery. No, this is not meant to be amusing. If you want to be great at a sport of some kind, you would watch it, talk to others who do it, join in on opportunities to participate in it, and spend as much time as possible around the players, wouldn't you? Cemeteries are wonderful because they have four major helpful qualifications:

A—The Disincarnate's physical remains are there. Headstones and all manner of signifiers of the culture of death are there. Your mind will be with death while you are there and you are now tuned up to the work at hand.

B—The sorrow is there. **Sorrow is a powerful physical force**. The land is fertilized with tears from crying, mourning survivors. While there, on that ground, you stand on a physical manifestation of transition, sorrow, loss and a host of other powerful pulsing emotions. You, as a Sorcerer, will absorb the power of that sorrow. This is why there are Sorcery Events listed herein where the instructions include cutting open the bottom of your feet.

C—The Disincarnate are consistently baited by sadness. They walk and try to make contact with anyone who can, and is willing, to see and hear them. This is a powerful opportunity for you to tune into random Disincarnates and communicate with them, or at least acknowledge their presence. Every time you do this it tunes you up a bit more to practice Necromancy. You will find through these unplanned interactions that the randomness provides you with abilities that cannot be obtained in any other way. These are very valuable moments.

D—Modern cemeteries are, by and large, well cared for. By contrast, more ancient cemeteries are often left to evolve into wonderful new places, with crumbling headstones and overgrown vegetation, in a way changing into places of antiquity where the pallor of the place, not the presence of the Disincarnate, define it. Disincarnate visit them for other reasons. **Modern cemeteries are most often the place where The Living Tend To The Dead!** It is unique insomuch as the Disincarnates **EXPECT** this attention there. Exploit that expectation. Sit with them, amongst them, ask for an agreement, and listen. Take the time to watch carefully as well. As you begin to see and hear them, open your skin with lancets in several places and BAIT them with the smell of your life force. Enjoy the communication. Close this portal by taking a keepsake from no fewer than three graves, including one from a child, and tell them you will return.

5. Portal on an Altar To Yourself

Create an Altar To Yourself by portraying your strengths. Let your ego guide you in its construction and embellishment. Keep many dried, preserved bits of your sacred Elixir on it, mixed into items you have collected from the dead. Learn to be comfortable in front of it and do not be embarrassed by having photos of yourself, awards, and that which reminds you of your accomplishments. Allow it to be a place you can use for Necromancy whenever you need to. BLEED YOURSELF on it every day until it works for you. Choose harvest locations that feel right for you. This type of altar can become a vessel toward the opening of an Eternal Portal.

Rituals to Open Eternal Portals

Living with an Eternal Portal is much like donating a kidney. Yes, you may function fine with just one but you will always be more susceptible to Death.

NOTE:

THE OPENING OF ETERNAL PORTALS

CANNOT BE REVERSED.

When someone donates a kidney to another human being, they have made an agreement that to achieve this goal they will always be slightly closer to Death, slightly less whole, and forever vulnerable. That vulnerability is very tempting to the dead. People have reported to me that they see or hear their deceased ancestors after donating blood. Recently I have spoken to two kidney donors, several kidney recipients, and a number of bone marrow donors. They each have had a heightened awareness of the presence of the Disincarnate. One of them has become a Necromancer.

Opening an Eternal Portal means that you have chosen Necromancy above all else as your life's work. Returning to the kidney donor example, even if the donor received a new, second kidney, their body would never be the same after two major surgeries and the time spent functioning on one kidney only.

Living eternally in life amongst the Disincarnate creates that forever damage that can never be completely reversed or undone. A Necromancer lives with that Eternal Portal and is always just closer to death than other living humans. Everything I have written about Momentary Portals will no longer matter if you go this route. We will not really be discussing natural ability because that is a given. No Eternal Portal will open for you without it. These are tolls, skills, steps to blow open the ability you must already have, and taking these steps will prove that one way or the other.

I caution you...do not test the Disincarnate. If you are taking these steps to see if this is your path, as some sort of experiment, then stop right now. Once they know you can hear them, pulling out will be like looking over your shoulder forever. You will be a fugitive. If you are taking these steps because you cannot imagine a life lived any other way and you want this more than any kind of normal, sane, safe life, then proceed on this path.

Take a clear inventory of your motives. If you seek these skills because you have the ability and desire to walk in the dark amongst those you may not even be able to see, and who may want any number of tasks from you, and who, apparently no longer have anything to lose, then continue. If you want this path with absolute conviction, no one will be able to talk you out of it. Lastly, if you want to continuously be perceived as a nut, charlatan, roadside psychic, side-show freak—if that's the life you want—then read on.

RITUAL PACES TO THE ETERNAL PORTAL

There is no thing such as "self initiation" in Sorcery as it is the harnessing of that which is within. To whom would we be taking an oath? Save that nonsense for the earth religion types. Sorcery is a solitary art, even if you do it in a room with other Sorcerers. In the presence of the Left Hand we are naturally solitary when using our own power. All one can do is make an agreement with oneself to participate fully in the ritual at hand. You have either made this agreement or not. **No one is initiated**. Create a Creed so that you have developed a strong contract with Death and the Disincarnate and begin the work, as you already have all the components in your Blood vessels.

Your commitment will make it clear. The Disincarnate either want to work with you or not. That being said, there is a period of ritual which shows the Disincarnate that you are not turning back, that you are willing to enter this oddly abusive way of life, and that you accept that this is much like donating a kidney. The damage is permanent.

Put the "Take 21 Days" chapter that follows into action. It is—as is this entire "grimoire"—a suggestion only. I will tell you that it has been tried, it works, and therefore has proven to get the attention of the Disincarnate. It has proven that the agreement is unbreakable.

TAKE 21 DAYS

......that is my suggestion. Anything you do for twenty-one days you will most likely do in full consciousness. During that time:

- Collect artifacts and belongings of the dead
- Gather and carry grave dirt
- Create a significant storage of your Sacred Elixir, wet and dry
- Test Sigils, research them, create them, experience them
- Create the following incense:

Elixir Incense

Formula:

(Note: Except for the Elixir itself, this and my other incense formulas do not specify exact measurements. Incense is like a finely tuned instrument; you just know when it is spot-on correct, pleasing...)

1. Lay down some wormwood powder (spread some out in a non-porous mixing dish)
2. Add no fewer than seven drops of your Sacred Elixir harvested at this moment (from wherever you feel would be the *least* comfortable area that you could tolerate)
3. Add benzion (styrax) in powder form chipped away from a block and ground
4. Add graveyard dirt or graveyard dust

Make this incense as often as needed to burn every night for at least twenty-one nights.

- Light candles every night anointed with your Sacred Elixir. This process will help you to learn to appreciate, and ultimately to crave, the scent of your own Sacred Elixir mixing with the fire. It is applied physics. The heat applied to your Sacred Elixir involves your Elixir in the heat transfer creating Sacred Elixir-driven energy.
- Spend as many hours as possible sitting in quiet, listening and asking the Disincarnate to talk to you. Invite them in.
- Denounce all you have been asked to believe about the ways and limitations of relationships between the living and the Dead.
- Make an altar to your own power and fill it with images, Elixir and pride objects.
- Expect some people to walk out of your life.
- Lie down on graves. If possible sleep in a cemetery or in a Mausoleum.
- Don't ask for opinions or talk about these twenty-one days with non-practitioners.
- Allow your mind to have thoughts about the dying process and how that experience may feel. (These do NOT involve suicidal thoughts, but rather allowing yourself to see the process from the point of view of the deceased.)
- Observe sorrow. Attend wakes and burials. They are usually listed on websites, obituaries, and burial schedules at cemeteries.
- Avoid watching TV or film for these twenty-one days. Stay only in the story of the work.

I think I have made my point about the importance of spending twenty-one days amongst Death. Now feel free to go back and look over the "Sorcery Events" chapter. Perform an Event and you will see a better outcome than you had experienced before you spent the 21 days realigning.

INACCESSIBLE DEATH

Death is everywhere. In many parts of the world the problem for students of Necromancy is that Death is treated as a young, protected child, hidden and untouchable. I've spent so many years amongst the dead that I wonder, for all of you, if the challenge is to be able to raise them or to even get access to them at all. Our modern way of Death turns the body of the newly deceased into an icon, an inaccessible relic kept sacred behind closed doors. This makes it quite difficult for Necromancers to do the vital rituals needed to make a solid Eternal Portal. I stress the point that you cannot do this work if you have not closed your eyes and fallen into a deep sleep amongst the Dead. In that moment you must let go of fear so completely that you have not a shred of worry that Death will take you. Instead you strive to be in possession of a deep and profound desire that Death WILL enter with you into a partnership—that of a mentor to a willing, unknowing disciple.

Angela's Grandmother

When I was twelve years old, a classmate, Angela, told me that when her grandmother was brought home from the hospital, she overheard her mother say that the old woman was coming home to die. I was fascinated. I had to see it happen. I had to be there, be a witness. I became obsessed with seeing Death come and whisk this ancient woman away.

I knew in the sensible part of my mind that if I phrased it quite that way, I would not be granted that opportunity. I thought about it carefully. I tell this story because I must express to you what must be done. Lie. Pretend. Cheat. Do whatever is necessary to watch Death in all of Death's steps, abilities and phases. With that in mind, I came up with two possibilities that would allow me access to Angela's dying Grandmother. Angela often showed an interest in two areas: getting money for shopping and the traditions of my Sicilian family. So I made up a magnificent lie that wealth will come to those who have a Sicilian girl in the house when a death occurs. I went on to cite many family examples (all stories I made up as I went along) in a blatant effort to extort what I desired from the situation. I told Angela that I would do this favor for her for ten percent of the money that would magically come to her soon after the old lady died. I told her that what I was proposing was actually a job, that every Sicilian family had someone who did this work. So no one got suspicious, I said it was usually a child.

Angela was thrilled and expressed to her not-very-maternal mother that she could not get through the process of losing her Grandmom (as she was an only child) without a friend in the house she could talk to. Her mother, just happy that Angela would leave her alone, said yes. My parents felt much the same way and were happy to be rid of me for a multi-night sleep over. Everyone, but most of all me, got exactly what they desired—so far.

Three nights later I was holding poor Angela's hand as a priest with a brogue was giving last rites—the sacrament known as Extreme Unction—to Grandma. I placed my other hand on Grandma's shoulder. She creakily opened her dying eyelids and rolled her yellowing eyes towards me. The nearly-dead are gifted, I have come to notice, with momentary wisdom of what is occurring in the living-place they are leaving. Others in the room reported her dying glance at me as gratitude that a friend would support her dear granddaughter. But I knew that with her glance she was asking me if I was enjoying the show.

I did not move my hand from that dying old woman's body. I stood still. I breathed in as Grandma breathed out for the last time, taking in my first breath of a natural human death, as an ancient, ninety-seven year old human died.

This title I bestowed upon myself—The Necromancer—has always been mine, since the day I was conceived.

It turns out, as the pure Sorcery of a rare child Necromancer would, it was the trifecta of Death. Read on.

After having the opportunity to absorb Grandma's death, I was told there would be an in-home funeral. Grandma was laid out in their ample Victorian living room with an open casket for three days and nights. I sat near the casket as often as I could, sneaked down at night to do so, until I felt the full process had occurred and Death had HAPPENED. The moment I felt that this body was no longer in process, which was somewhere toward the end of the second night, then I was just in it for the end process.

Grandma also left Angela some money, which she shared with me as per my agreement. Angela didn't know that as far as I was concerned I had already been paid quite well by the experience alone.

Over the next few years I was actually asked to do this a few more times as the story took on legs of its own. Thus the life of the Necromancer...

FIVE RITUALS INVOLVING ADDITIONAL MATERIALS

These five rituals are constructed in ways that involve materials not spoken about in the "Sorcery Events" chapter. They represent a brief look into additional methods of Blood Sorcery, and are often requested by clients and students. I thought carefully, recalling those rituals about which I receive the most inquiries. These are those five rituals.

Each of the chosen rituals had to fall into all of the following categories:

A. The ritual had to be basic enough to be done by someone who was new to Blood Sorcery as long as they were fully committed to the work.
B. The ritual had to be relevant enough that even an adept would continue to use it in their practice.
C. The ritual could **not** produce a fatal or near fatal outcome or a permanent physical distortion as those are directives only given to my students and/or clients who have gained my trust. They are performed under the most cautious guidelines, **as to take a life a Blood Sorcerer makes a very particular sacrifice (and gains a very particular facet)** and this is not the book in which to discuss those particular rituals.

1. Blocking the "Work" of Another from Affecting You

There are three ways to do this. One I will discuss only with Sorcerers in person; another I will share only with my students and fellow Sorcerers; and this one—which works extraordinarily well, but brings us to the subject of animal sacrifice.

Here is what I find puzzling: you will call an exterminator to rid your home of vermin, eat in restaurants serving the freshest meats, crush a bug on a sidewalk, and even feed live mice to your pets. You wear leather, use horn and bone buttons, but the collective you recoils at animal sacrifice.

For this ritual you will have to decide if it is better to be a victim at the hand of someone's work (Sorcery, gossip, personal or professional sabotage, etc., all apply here), or if you are willing to kill a rodent to make it stop. This is Sorcery and sometimes someone has to suffer to relieve suffering—it is up to you.

Collect any and all images, signatures, clothing, any scrap of anything the low-life human who is working against you has touched. Obtaining a biological would be the ultimate component but is not always possible. If this is a former lover, have sex with them first and use their body fluids— Sorcery is no simple game—or ask someone else to do that for you (no, you did NOT misread that).

Buy a rat. Put it in a tank or box. Do not feed it for twenty-four hours. Give it only a bit of water so it will not die. Shred the collected materials from the person you are working and mix them with peanut butter. Smear the mix on a cracker. Using paint or a marker or nail polish or ink, write the name of your enemy/detractor on the rat's back starting at the tail end and finishing at the top of the head between the eyes.

Place the cracker in the rat's enclosure. Let the rat eat the cracker. Remove the rat from the tank (be careful, they bite and fight—use a mouse if you can't manage a rat and consider leather gloves), and with one simple motion (I suggest a well-sharpened cleaver) cut its head off. When the body stops wiggling, cut off the tail and squeeze a few drops into some red ink. (BONUS: Let the tail dry for a day or so and use it as a paintbrush or writing utensil the next time you are doing a sigil or note for revenge or justice Sorcery.) Place a few drops of your Sacred Elixir into the same red, rat-blood ink and add one drop of black ink to the mix. With your quill write the following on pure white cotton/linen paper:

"I am no longer affected by you, I am in control of you as I am writing the very words you read with ink of your remains."

When the ink dries, bury the note in ground your detractor lives on or walks over every day. If there is any remaining ink, keep it refrigerated and use it the next time you wish to do this sort of sorcery on someone and cannot get any of their belongings. It is better than not having anything to work with. As an added bonus, and if the opportunity arises, show the rat tail to the detractor without saying one single word.

IT IS DONE—THERE IS BLOOD ON IT.

2. Opening Up Your Ability to Learn This Work

First read through this entire book.

Obtain several dozen small vials. They are easily obtained from oil vendors. Go through the list of locations from which to draw the Elixir. Over several days, using lancets, take many tiny samples. Absorb them (dots of the Elixir) onto bits of fabric or cotton/linen paper, always clean and unused. Get a fresh, never before used journal. Smear each puncture into the journal and write a note about the very first image or thought that comes to you during that puncture. Put the swab in a vial, number them in order, and continue in this fashion until you begin to hear comments from the Disincarnate about your thoughts. It could take a day, a year; it is different for everyone.

Once the voices begin and you can communicate with them, wrap all the vials in a piece of linen or cotton and hide them away. At a future time, this will be a powerful survival tool but that is the subject of another writing concerning demons, and for sharing with my students. Continue the use of the journal to detail your Sorcery Events.

3. Reversing Loss to Gain

Rip pieces of linen into strips as if you were making mummy wrappings. I suggest you work with four-inch wide pieces. Wrap them around your left forearm starting at the elbow and working toward the wrist. Sew them closed so they do not unwrap on their own. You will not be bathing during this time. For three sunrises, using a lancet, poke into your outer forearm (hair side) no fewer than three times, and observe as the Sacred Elixir turns the natural linen color to red.

On the sunset of the third day, cut away the stitches and remove the wrap. Within the next hour perform an act thought of as decadent or taboo, keeping the wrap with you, but well hidden.

Transfer the wrap, inside out, to your right forearm wrapping in the same manner as before. Throughout the night, puncture through the linen with a lancet, allowing left-side Elixir to mix with the dried Elixir. Puncture as often as you feel you need to, but no fewer than five times and no greater than eighty-eight times. Allow all Elixir to dry. Remove the wrap, roll it up and while keeping it with you, sexually gratify yourself, smearing a spot of biologicals from your sexual gratification onto the right and left Elixirs dried together.

Keep the linen with you until the next sundown. Snip off a piece that contains all three liquids.

Keep that piece with you somewhere against the skin of the right side of your body. Before dusk, place yourself upon a grave of someone who appears to have had very little means. Bring yourself to tears at the thought of THEIR suffering (not *yours*). Wipe your tears with the large piece of linen, mixing your tears with the other three biologicals.

Immediately bury the wrap at the base of their headstone and RUN away from the grave. Remain silent for no fewer than three hours. Approach the most attractive stranger you can find and tell them they are ugly or difficult to look at. Store the small piece of linen from the right side of your body in the left sleeve of something you have not worn while doing this ritual. All these seemingly bizarre tasks are readjusting reality, causing a new truth.

Go nap until you naturally arise. Then shower. Expect to see loss change to gain.

4. Asking the Disincarnate to Intercede

Use this Sorcery Event if you are dealing with a difficult situation involving someone who will not listen to your side of an argument. This is helpful with **LEGAL matters** as well.

Collect a non-biological, pride-based item, such as a business card, stationery or an original signature, or a photo where the person in question was posing for or smiling for the camera. The best situation is if it comes from their own hand, such as a business card they gave directly to you.

Collect grave dirt from five unrelated Disincarnate and mix them together with red wine and eight drops of your Sacred Elixir taken from inside the right side of your mouth. Make the mixture loose as if you are making paint. Make a paintbrush from either the hair of your own head (right side) OR from hair from a lover who you left by your own choice. **(It is always a good plan for Sorcerers to collect things as they go along in life.)** Wrap the hair around a twig from a cemetery or a stem from a dead, red rose and mix the ingredients with the other end of the twig or stem. Secure the hairs with thread wrapped many times.

On a clean piece of cotton paper (or parchment or other entirely organic paper), paint the following image:

Carry it for twenty-four hours, treating it with great care. Let it believe it is very important to you. Then suddenly set fire to it and pour some of the remaining liquid over it in a place where people will walk on it or animals may pee on it.

Go put flowers on the grave of someone who seems forgotten. Call the person you have done Sorcery on and tell them you have done Sorcery on them (no details!) and you no longer care what they think.

They will begin to communicate with you. Silently thank the Disincarnate who stepped in to be part of this Sorcery Event—even though you do not know them—and end the communication while the person is still attempting communication with you no matter what method they are using to respond.

5. Attainment:
Use for Fertility and Career Advancements

As Sacred Elixir Sorcerers it would be advantageous if you obtained human bones. They can be purchased. There is no more or less power in various bones, only different types of power. Although human skulls are quite dramatic, they are not the most powerful bone. They are in fact a collection of bones, each with a different energy and mood. I am a fan of human finger bones and two other bones in particular. To do the most efficient Attainment Sorcery it is wise to use human bone as the first choice.

Attainment Sorcery is really Containment Sorcery, by which I mean one must work the physical energy to bring what is desired into a designed and SPECIFIC place to be collected from the source by the rightful owner.

Using a bone, preferably human, tap out a circle and sit inside of it. Say:

KETET PESCITARE MODIKETT FULCRUM

Again, the words are not an ancient Latin phrase so save your research time. Speaking these "words" in a low, vibrating voice activates the Sorcery Event. I found these words by listening to the feedback from specific Disincarnate and one of my attending Demons.

Doing this will lock you in (or out, as you will say at the end of this step and keep out distraction. Stay in the circle until you can see what you want quite clearly. Using a lancet, cut a letter that represents your desire into your left palm. Suction your mouth around the letter and drink you own Elixir from the incision. Swallow twice and the third time spit the sucked out Sacred Elixir onto the bone. Say the words again and leave your circle, bringing the bone with you. If your palm still bleeds, just let it.

Allow the bone to sit and dry for a while. Using a sharp knife, scrape off the Sacred Elixir along with some bone shavings. (It is helpful to do this into a paper bag so the bits do not jump away and get lost.) Grind the bits down with a mortar and pestle until they are as fine as they can be and mix them with black ink. Put the mixture in a small jar or vial and tuck it inside a mausoleum. Let it spend three nights sleeping amongst the dead. Return to the spot and open the jar. Shake it and, using your left ring finger, make a single smear of the ink on the floor of the mausoleum; leave a clear fingerprint at both the beginning and the end of the smear. Bring home the jar and sleep with it in your bed. As you are lying in your bed, invite the inhabitants of the mausoleum that hosted your ink to sleep with you this one night. Allow yourself to drift, to believe you are experiencing the death of an individual in that mausoleum. Negotiate an agreement with that individual such that they assist you toward that which you wish to attain, and in exchange you give that individual the opportunity to speak through you or live through you for a specific number of hours. Negotiate carefully as the disincarnate are often desperate to get back into the experience of living. Define strong boundaries of what you will or will not do and where you will or will not go. When you feel the agreement is made, using the ink and a fresh quill or nib, write the details of the agreement on clean cotton or linen paper and sign it. Leave the pen and the ink available for the Disincarnate to sign as well. You will find they often make a mark of some kind.

Sleep and when you awake you will find additional marks on the document, as you have been baiting the Disincarnate with inky Elixir and bone for three nights and they are not likely to resist.

Keep the ink for additional agreements. It is very powerful. The individual will make itself known to you when it is time to use it again in future Sorcery Events, as you now have a relationship with this particular disincarnate. The next day return the agreement to the mausoleum and leave it there. It belongs to them. You will attain that which you desire.

CORPOREAL NECROMANCY

TECHNIQUES OF SURVIVAL AMONGST THE DISINCARNATE

Corporeal Necromancy—Any method of Necromancy which involves a human body, either actually from the disincarnate at issue, or a replacement body intended for re-inhabitation.

WARNING

THIS SECTION INVOLVES EXTREME WORK AND CONTROL OF THE SACRED ELIXIR. NONE OF THIS WORK IS MEANT FOR MINORS OR PERSONS IMPAIRED BY MENTAL ILLNESS OR THOSE WITH SUICIDAL TENDENCIES.

In order to walk amongst the dead, the Sorceress must possess an understanding of the power inherent in Blood's scent and how to disguise it. Consider this imagery. If you are in the woods and you hear the howl of a wolf, will fear save you? No, it will not. Will fear serve you? No, it will not. What is your strategy for self-preservation? Should you make slits all over your body and let the wolves catch your scent on the wind? This is obviously not a good strategy. Do you climb a tree and hope to make it until morning, when the wolves are less likely to hunt? That may work, but it isn't a guarantee as wolves' behavior is not based on our expectations of them. You don't know or understand their howls, so what to do?

If you bleed, if you become injured and your Sacred Elixir escapes, understand that a wolf's nose picks up a zillion tiny particles of information and your blood is a magnet for their attentions.

Scent Suppression

The benefits would be substantial if you could control your scent by communicating with your blood, requesting that is recede from your skin's surface, training it to pull its scent deep within. What if you could speak to the metals in your body and smell like iron or copper rather than meat? The scenario above is an excellent example of an appropriate and advantageous time to have the skill of Scent Suppression. **Scent Suppression is the tool that allows Necromancers to walk amongst the Dead undetected, enjoying the privileged of hearing their thoughts without their perception of incarnate interruption. More simply put**—this is how we spy on them, how we protect ourselves from the most dangerous of them, how we live amongst Demons and learn their secrets.

To learn to create Scent Suppression you must understand how the liquid that is your Blood works, how it travels in the body, and how that relates to keeping the bulk of your Blood away from the surface of your skin.

I HAVE DISCOVERED A CONNECTION BETWEEN THE TECHNIQUES OF TONIC IMMOBILITY AND THE MAMMALIAN DIVE REFLEX AND THE NECROMANCER'S NEED FOR SCENT SUPPRESSION.

I bring this information to the reader at this point to explain Scent Suppression so the living can walk amongst the dead and not be detected. This book embraces the Science of Sorcery and these facts support the theory of Scent Suppression as each of these phenomena involve Blood moving from a topical zone (skin) to a deeper zone (muscles and organs). The natural outcome of these acts is a reduction in the availability of the scent of our Blood by others......all others.

Mammalian Dive Reflex

The Mammalian Dive Reflex is a phenomenon that occurs amongst diving mammals. It comprises a set of changes that allow for extended depth and duration dives under extreme pressures. This technique, which optimizes respiration, allows for extended underwater activities. The diving reflex is triggered specifically by cold water contacting the face. Prior to 1948, the Mammalian Dive Reflex phenomenon had been studied in seals, dolphins, penguins and whales. The advent of human exploration of deep breath-hold dives produced evidence that this reflex exists in humans as well. Given that humans were not built for deep breath-hold dives, it is an interesting finding that humans can produce this reflex.

There are three effects:

Bradycardia is the first response to submersion. Immediately upon facial contact with cold water, the human heart rate slows down ten to twenty-five percent.

Peripheral Vasoconstriction then sets in. When under high pressure induced by deep diving, capillaries in the extremities start closing off, stopping blood circulation to those areas. Note that vasoconstriction usually applies to arterioles, but in this case is completely an effect of the capillaries. Toes and fingers close off first, then hands and feet, and ultimately arms and legs stop allowing blood circulation, leaving more blood for use by the heart and brain.

Blood Shift is the part of the phenomenon that most specifically assists Necromancers with safe passage amongst the dead. Blood Shift occurs only during very deep dives. When this happens, organ and circulatory walls allow plasma/water to pass freely throughout the thoracic cavity so its pressure stays constant. As a result, the organs aren't crushed by the **excess Blood pulling further from the surface and limbs and filling the organs and interstitial spaces** as they press against the pressure of the water. **This is the point at which Mammalian Dive Reflex crosses into use with Scent Suppression and is useful to Necromancers.** If we could train our bodies to mimic this experience before undertaking walks amongst the dead we would stand a better chance of not being detected or at least not being detected as soon. This is vital to create a safe environment for travel in these areas just as deer hunters strive to suppress their scents in order to not lose the opportunity for a kill and to avoid attack by defensive prey. Hunters use chemicals and suits that suppress scent. For the purpose of walking amongst the Disincarnate in a hostile environment, we must be able to Scent Suppress on demand.

Tonic Immobility

Tonic immobility, aka Apparent Death, is a natural state of paralysis that animals enter, in most cases when presented with a threat. Some scientists relate it to mating in certain animals like the shark.

Some sharks can be placed in a tonic state by flipping them over and exposing them fully belly side up. The shark remains in this state of paralysis for an average of fifteen minutes before it recovers. Scientists have exploited this phenomenon to study shark behavior and create a chemical shark repellent from the findings of the chemical process of Tonic Immobility.

Tonic Immobility is an adaptive response that may occur to avoid a predator when one does not perceive the possibility of winning a fight. As predators often react to even the most subtle movement, if the prey remains immobile instead of struggling or fighting or running, the probability of escaping increases. Most predators are not wired to eat what they do not have to kill, so they lose interest.

This adaptive faux death may also be helpful in the process of traversing amongst the Disincarnate.

Consider a scenario where you, as the Necromancer, have decided that you must not only open a portal, but also pass through one and be in the presence of the dead to obtain information or skills required for a Sorcery Event. In that case, it could be extraordinarily dangerous for you to traverse amongst those Disincarnate who do not know you, can see you, smell your blood, and are resentful of your living status. They may take your life in hope that doing so will restore their life status. If in that situation you could slow your heartbeat and pull your blood away from your skin (**Mammalian Dive Reflex**), your scent would drop off and your pallor would go mildly anoxic (diminished surface oxygen) creating a blue cast upon your skin: an un-living pallor. The outcome would afford you the look and scent of death. In that situation if you felt that any of the disincarnate in your presence might sense you are living, an ability to spontaneously induce **Tonic Immobility** would probably be enough to make you seem believably dead.

EXERCISE YOUR ABILITY TO INDUCE
TONIC IMMOBILITY AND THE MAMMALIAN DIVE REFLEX

Awareness of the skills that are necessary, and learning to develop these skills are two very different experiences. It is best if, while learning these skills, you can develop a relationship with one disincarnate whom you can trust. Experiment with various skills and ask that particular disincarnate if they can see and smell the changes. **Do not walk amongst unknown disincarnates if you cannot be sure that you have mastered the skill of Scent Suppression.** If you cannot

establish a relationship with one disincarnate who is willing
to help you critique your progress, then you are not ready
to walk amongst graves of others.

Exercise in the Induction of Tonic Immobility

To induce Tonic Immobility work yourself into a state of
emotional shut-down utilizing a memory of an emotion or
an extreme trauma. Keep in mind that this is an exercise so
prepare ahead of time to bring yourself back through a
timer or warning bell. Note the physiological changes you
experience as your body moves from agitation to surrender.
The ability to induce this effect is the experience of Tonic
Immobility. Continue working in this manner, with a complete recuperation between attempts until you can induce
the chemical experience without resorting to the use of
devices such as memories of emotional trauma. That is the
goal. **Chemistry—not memory.**

Exercise in the Induction of Mammalian Dive Reflex

**DO NOT DO THIS EXERCISE IF YOU ARE NOT IN GOOD
HEALTH OR IF YOU HAVE OR HAVE HAD ANY
CARDIAC DISEASE. IF YOU ARE NOT PHYSICALLY FIT
ENOUGH FOR DIVING DO NOT DO THIS EXERCISE.**

---

1. Create a chart by noting your resting pulse every hour
for six hours. Find the average.
2. Cold water is a stimulus for Mammalian Dive Reflex.
Fill a bowl that can accommodate your face, and take your
pulse before you begin. The anticipation of the exercise may
increase your heartbeat. If that happens use the resting
heartbeat from your data. Place the bowl on a table. Sit on a
stable chair facing the bowl. Take a deep breath and lower

your face into the bowl. Stay for as long as you can comfortably hold your breath. Remove your face from the cold water and take your pulse. Continue this exercise daily until you can feel the slowing of your heartbeat via this method.

3. Once you have pulse data from no fewer than two dozen of these exercises, broaden the scope of this exercise by diving into a cold pool. When the water hits your face, take note of the *physical changes* your body is experiencing. The ability to induce these changes without the "tool" of cold water contacting your face will afford you the skill to spontaneously induce Tonic Immobility.

CATEGORIES OF CORPOREAL NECROMANCY

This is a partial list of types of Corporeal Necromancy. The actual ritual methods to accomplish these types of Necromancy will be extensively covered in the forthcoming book, *Demonworks, The Stygian Manual.*

1. **Lifting/Actual**—This method allows the Sorcerer to reanimate the physical body of the disincarnate, placing the living energy back into the SAME body it has left. This is the most complicated form of Corporeal Necromancy. There are multiple conditions to consider before attempting this "Lift"; The condition of the body, length of time since the recognized time of death, embalming or other post mortem procedures such as autopsy or the harvesting of organs intended for donation. Finally, the willingness of the disincarnate to re-inhabit this body is vital to the process. Forced "lifting" is a manner by which one can create demons, and not the material for this volume.

2. **Reassignment/Re-inhabitation**—Reassigning the Disincarnate into an existing body other than their own. I also refer to this as **POST MORTEM POSSESSION** which is accomplished by making the acquaintance of someone who is on Death's doorstep. I specifically refer to someone whose functional body is in those final few seconds of participating in life. This situation may make the opportunity attractive to a Disincarnate who still has enough sense memory of being corporeal. That Disincarnate will step into the body. This is my explanation for the sightings of so many Disincarnate in hospitals and at disaster sites.

Perhaps when someone claims they went through a tunnel and someone told them to **Go Back**, a Disincarnate seeking a new vessel stops the body from dying long enough to remain active—physiology intact—(which is vital) with the intention of Post Mortem Possession.

The resulting reassignment will appear to be the original owner of the body, but in fact is the new inhabitant. Confusion will continue until a settling has occurred. Settlings are a significant step in Re-inhabitation and will be discussed further in the forthcoming book, *Demonworks The Stygian Manual.*

3. **Fertility**—Intentional Re-entry, the disincarnate returns in a newly formed human. This can be accomplished in-utero with consent.

4. **Invoking**—When the disincarnate makes a plea to a Sorcerer to become reanimated and together they search for an impending birth and "hijack" the newborn for possession.

EXORCISM

I will address Exorcism in a thorough manner in my forthcoming book, *Demonworks, The Stygian Manual.* That being said, the cautionary tale continues here for those of you who seek an understanding of what is required to perform an Exorcism. My advice to you (which you will most likely not take), is **Do Not**, as a novice in this work, attempt an exorcism. A Demon that is trapped or chooses to be trapped in a human is in one of two states of being:

1. The Demon is either enraged at having been trapped, or
2. The Demon is filled with an egomaniacal power derived from having gotten into and taken over a human being.

Either way, its power can multiply a hundredfold and the Demon will kill you if you get it wrong while attempting to Exorcize it from the human or location it inhabits. Exorcisms are for those of us who have confronted Demons hundreds of times and removed them from locations against their will when they, not us, were in the comfort zone—and by all reason we should not have been the winner.

Exorcisms are to be done by those of us who understand that fear is an open wound that the demon will see as an opportunity to fill with its viral spit. Those of us who know this know it not only on an intellectual level, but also through experience.

WHAT IS *NOT* IN THIS BOOK

This is not an extensive work on demons, attending demons, exorcism, physical resurrection of the Dead, transferring the Disincarnate into a living human, dis-attachment, reassignment or implanting oneself or the disincarnate in physical or dream realms. Although I touch on some of those areas, **many of those things will be covered in the second book in this series**. I did not include, or in some cases expand upon these topics, because either these are techniques I only share with my students and/or some techniques cannot be shared via this format, as they need to be taught through example and or demonstration.

I also chose not to include how to keep others too ill to be in the way or how to manipulate lawyers and jurors as these techniques are my specialties—and it would be ridiculous to give that away.

Sorcery Events resulting in long-term damage of a physical or psychological nature, or death, are not taught in Book One, as they are subjects for further study. The ability to perform Sorcery by moving energy and materials by the wave of a hand or through glances is also not for this first book on the subject. Lastly, I teach some of these areas only to a select, inner group of students.

IF YOU WISH TO STUDY WITH ME, CONTACT ME DIRECTLY AND WE WILL HAVE A DISCUSSION. A DISCUSSION IS NOT AN AGREEMENT. THAT IS HOW IT BEGINS...

THE WORK OF THE FUTURE

THE PLATFORM

(Copyright 2010; Trademark Pending)

The Platform is a Blood Sorcery and Necromancy Laboratory—in a loosely hung version of what a laboratory can be. It is a space, an assemblage of usable components in the areas of physics, metallurgy, electric current, Tesla research, and working with magnets as these materials apply to Blood Sorcery. The Platform is a large room, slightly below ground level, with an iron floor. The Surface is a standable floor area and raised area comprised of magnets of extraordinary strength.

"The Sacred Elixir (Blood) within the human body contains enough iron to make a nail." We are, by that qualification, part of the magnetic equation as magnets are by definition that which is attracted to iron. Exploring this phenomenon from the physics perspective of Blood Sorcery is the main focus of my research at The Platform.

How does The Platform research pertain to Necromancy?

THE PLATFORM is set against the back wall of a large cemetery. Necromancy will be explored via this opportunity in conjunction with its connection to the Science of Sorcery. Necromancy will be approached from various methods, such as electric impulse study and usage of iron and magnetic enhancement. Through this exploration the focus will be fourfold:

First and foremost, to enhance communication between living and disincarnate individuals in the general sense with frequency and clarity.

The second focus is to create an environment of shared experiences as a group of living individuals communicating at the same time with a particular disincarnate. The goal is communication amongst a group of living humans, all able to see and hear the same Disincarnate. This experience will yield additional information and clarity through shared observation.

The third focus is to create an environment in which the communication with and from the Disincarnate can be documented via the collection and accumulation of audio and visual data.

The fourth focus, and perhaps the one that I personally find to be the most intriguing, is to establish a method by which the Disincarnate can freely leave communications for the living at any time via a number of permanently opened channels such as recorded image and audio, writing or the manipulation of letter tiles and other objects.

THE PLATFORM IS A LABORATORY FOR THE LIVING AND THE DEAD.

Additional Explorations

What of Sigils, candles, linen wraps, burials and the other more familiar components of Blood Sorcery? What if the concept of magnetism were infused into the work through these and other objects? Could the outcome produce data proving that Sorcery hits its intended target?

An exploration of mummification, defining the timeline of Death and the relationship between physical remains and persistent forms of energy **specific** to an individual disincarnate will be an intrinsic part of the research at The Platform.

Magnetics enter the work in combination with usage of
multiple energy sources based on the focal point of The
Surface.

This is the work of the Science of Blood Sorcery, and that
which we will begin to explore at:

THE PLATFORM

THE PLATFORM is a creation of The Sorceress
Cagliastro. All of the work which occurs at THE PLATFORM
is protected under the copyright of THE PLATFORM and
THE SURFACE.

CLOSING NOTES

THIS BOOK IS A TALISMAN, USE IT WISELY.

DO NOT SHARE IT.

IF YOU HAVE ONE THEN EITHER USE IT OR NOT BUT DO SHARE IT WITH OTHERS.

Sacred Elixir Sorcery and Necromancy are not just arts—they are a connection to the Disincarnate by the one thing we all share. If there is only one Cultural Universal, it is that shared experience between us all of the reaction to the appearance of the Sacred Elixir.

Sorceress Cagliastro, The Necromancer

ABOUT THE AUTHOR

Blood Sorceress, Necromancer, Mummifier, Magnetic Sorcery researcher, teacher, author, lecturer, embalmer, forensic reconstructionist, and consigliere to the disincarnate, Sorceress Cagliastro has spent decades in service to the Integrity of the Deceased as a trade embalmer and in years of work at the Office of the Chief Medical Examiner. Her PR experience includes working directly with Sir Richard Branson as one half of his team of US publicists at Virgin Media.

World traveled, Cagliastro currently lives in America with her daughter Mahgdalen, husband David, craven Miss Ruth Roses, and a pack of dogs including: Dio'volo Cané, Luigi Cané and Rue Cané. She occasionally takes students at The PlatforM, her laboratory for Blood Sorcery Science and Mummification.

www.sorceresscagliastro.com
cagliastro@sorceresscagliastro.com

MORE BOOKS ON MAGIC

CONDENSED CHAOS
An Introduction to Chaos Magic
by Phil Hine

Foreword by Peter J. Carroll

"The most concise statement of the logic of modern magic. Magic, in the light of modern physics, quantum theory and probability theory is now approaching science. We hope that a result of this will be a synthesis so that science will become more magical and magic more scientific."
— William S. Burroughs, author of *Naked Lunch*

"… a tour de force."
— Ian Read, *Chaos International*

PSYBERMAGICK
Advanced Ideas in Chaos Magick
by Peter J. Carroll

Filled with practical techniques, *PsyberMagick* give you the means to undo the fallacy of "being" and reach "sideways" into imaginary time to accomplish magic(k). Done in the style of Aleister Crowley's Book of Lies, and humorously illustrated, this book is a must for all Chaoist and Western magicians.

"*PsyberMagick* will stimulate outrage, chaos, confusion, and insight. It is hard-core, in-your-face, state-of-the-art magick." — Alan Wicca

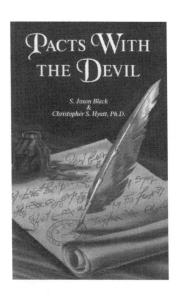

ISRAEL REGARDIE & THE PHILOSOPHER'S STONE

by Joseph C. Lisiewski, Ph.D.

Introduced by. Mark Stavish

Dr. Lisiewski delves into the hitherto unknown role Israel Regardie played in the world of Practical Laboratory Alchemy: not the world of idle speculation and so-called "inner alchemy," but the realm of the test tube and the Soxhlet Extractor. For the first time Dr. Regardie's private alchemical experiments are revealed as is his intense interaction with Frater Albertus of the Paracelsus Research Society and with the author himself.

KABBALISTIC CYCLES & THE MASTERY OF LIFE

by Joseph C. Lisiewski, Ph.D.

Foreword by Christopher S. Hyatt, Ph.D.

This groundbreaking book reveals a new system of occult cycles that gives you complete Control over your own life. The Kabbalistic Cycles System explains heretofore hidden universal laws known to but a few. The knowledge of these strange cycles— and the detailed, step-by-step explanation of their derivation and use—will place you light years beyond those who would maintain a stranglehold over you.

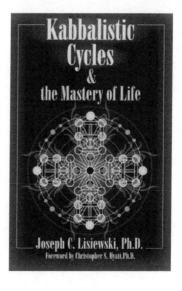

THE *Original* FALCON PRESS

Invites You to Visit Our Website:
http://originalfalcon.com

At our website you can:

- Browse the online catalog of all of our great titles
- Find out what's available and what's out of stock
- Get special discounts
- Order our titles through our secure online server
- Find products not available anywhere else including:
  - One of a kind and limited availability products
  - Special packages
  - Special pricing
- Get free gifts
- Join our email list for advance notice of New Releases and Special Offers
- Find out about book signings and author events
- Send email to our authors
- Read excerpts of many of our titles
- Find links to our authors' websites
- Discover links to other weird and wonderful sites
- And much, much more

Get online today at http://originalfalcon.com